# REPORT

## ON THE

# Excavations at Pataliputra

## (PATNA)

*THE PALIBOTHRA OF THE GREEKS*

L. A. WADDELL

PLATE I

(Frontispiece)

BUDDHIST STONE RAILING FROM PATALIPUTRA

Reduced to [illegible]

*Now in Indian Museum*

Photo by L.A. Waddell

Photogravure, Survey of India Offices, Calcutta April 1903

# REPORT

ON THE

# EXCAVATIONS AT PATALIPUTRA (PATNA)

*THE PALIBOTHRA OF THE GREEKS*

L. A. WADDELL

ISBN : 978-93-5324-575-7 (HB)

First Published, Calcutta, 1903

Published, 2020

*Published by*

Facsimile Publisher
12 Pragati Market
Ashok Vihar, Ph-2
Delhi-110052
E-mail: books@facsimilepublisher.com

*Printed at:* G. Print Process, Delhi.

**Report on the Excavations at Pataliputra (Patna)**

***The Palibothra of the Greeks***

Author: L. A. Waddell

# REPORT

ON THE

# EXCAVATIONS AT PĀTALIPUTRA (PATNA)

*THE PALIBOTHRA OF THE GREEKS.*

BY

L. A. WADDELL, M.B., LL.D.,

LIEUT.-COLONEL, INDIAN MEDICAL SERVICE.

CALCUTTA:

BENGAL SECRETARIAT PRESS.

1903.

# CONTENTS.

PAGE

HISTORICAL INTRODUCTION: FOUNDATION, DEVELOPMENT AND DECLINE OF PĀṬALIPUTRA . . . 1
SEARCH FOR THE LOST SITE . . . 9
DISCOVERY OF THE SITE . . . 11
EXCAVATIONS: . . . 16
THE CITY: ITS LOCATION AND BOUNDARIES . . . 19
THE CITY WALLS . . . 21
THE 'PALACE OF THE MAURYAS' . . . 24
SUMMARY OF RESULTS . . . 59

## APPENDICES.

I.—The *Mauryas* . . . 61
II.—Origin of Stone Building and Sculpture in Ancient India . . . 63
III.—Legend of the Founding of Pāṭaliputra . . . 65
IV.—Statues of its giant-builders . . . 67
V.—Descriptions of the city from Chinese records—
A.—By Fa Hian . . . 69
B.—By Hiuen Tsiang . . . 71
VI.—Legend of Asoka's Hell . . . 75
VII.—Report on the excavation of the great Stūpa by Mr. C. R. Wilson 77
VIII.—Upagupta, the High Priest of Asoka, and his identity with Mogalliputta Tissa of the Ceylonese . . . 80
IX.—Jain inscription translated by Dr. T. Bloch . . . 83

## ILLUSTRATIONS.

Plate I.—Buddhist Stone Railing . . . Frontispiece
" II.—Colossal Capital, *quasi*-Greek . . . To face p. 16
" III.—Archaic Stone Railing . . . " 34
" IV.—View of great Stūpa masonry . . . " 48
" V.—Inscription in Jain temple . . . " 56
Plan I.—Location of monuments according to Chinese descriptions " 12
" II.—Actual position of Ruins (10″ =1 mile) . . . " 28
" III.—Environs of *Asoka*-pillar . . . " 30
" IV.—Great Stūpa . . . " 48
Map of Pāṭaliputra . . . " 84

REPORT

ON THE

# EXCAVATIONS AT PĀṬALIPUTRA (PATNA),

## *THE PALIBOTHRA OF THE GREEKS,*

BY

L. A. WADDELL, M.B., LL.D.,

LIEUT.-COLONEL, INDIAN MEDICAL SERVICE.

---

"*Among famous places, busy marts and emporiums,* PĀṬALIPUTRA *will be the greatest; (but) three perils will threaten it—fire, water, and internal strife.*"—BUDDHA's prophecy in the Tibetan and other scriptures.[1]

HERCULES "*was the founder of no small number of cities, the most renowned and greatest of which he called* PALIBOTHRA."—Diodôrus the Sicilian, Hist., iii, 3.

THE 'Palibothra' of the Greeks, *Pāṭaliputra*, the 'City of sweet-scented flowers,' so famous in eastern legend and story, is historically of great importance.

Although it was not one of the very oldest cities of India, it was the seat of the most powerful ancient dynasties, and it has given us, through the narrative of a Greek ambassador to its court, our first fixed landmark in Indian chronology. Its buried ruins also doubtless still hide invaluable materials for reconstructing much of the lost history of early India, and especially for solving that important question as to the influence of the West upon the early civilization of Ancient India.

---

[1] *Mahāparinirvāṇa sūtra.*—ROCKHILL'S "Life of Buddha," 128. Also Pāli version *Vinaya pitakam* I, 26, transld. by DAVIDS in "Sacred Books of East," XI 17; and *Mahāvagga, VI*, 28, 7.

In these enquiries unfortunately owing to the almost total absence of anything like trustworthy information in the native 'histories' which consist mainly of tangled fable and conjecture of relatively modern composition, we have to work largely in the dark, and reconstruct even the outlines of the lost history, from other sources. We have to depend chiefly upon the testimony of inscriptions on stones, coins, etc., dug out of the ruins of the unknown past, and piecing together these fragmentary scraps of information by the inductive method of science, we have to supplement them by such stray references as may be found in Greek, Persian, Chinese, or other contemporary history, and may only use the Indian legendary material to fill in where it can a few blanks provisionally until more convincing evidence is forthcoming.

In the light of these researches, peering down the dark vistas of the past, we see that at the time of BUDDHA's visit, referred to in the above-quoted lines,—that is, somewhere between the fourth and fifth centuries before our era—*Pāṭaliputra* was a small village on the south bank of the Ganges, and it was being fortified by the king of *Rājagṛha* (*Rājgir*)[1] as a post from which he might conquer the adjoining provinces and petty republics across the river.

Standing at a point of such great commercial and strategical importance, at or near the confluence of all the five great rivers of Mid-India,[2] namely, the *Ganges*, the *Gogra*, the *Rāpti*, the *Gandak*, and the *Sōn*, as seen in the accompanying map, and commanding the traffic of these great water-ways of the richest part of India, it quickly grew into a great city, as was predicted.

Within about one generation after Buddha's visit the new monarch[3] left the old stronghold of *Rājgir*, on the eastern edge of the highlands of Central India, overlooking the rich Ganges

[1] AJĀTAŚATRU.—He was son of BIMBISĀRA, and became king eight years before BUDDHA's death :—TĀRANĀTHA's Tibetan *Hist. Indian Buddhism*; also Buddhist Scriptures.

[2] At FA HIAN's visit it was 1 *yojan*, or about 7 miles, below "the junction of the 5 rivers:" *see* Appendix IV.

[3] It was made the royal residence by UDĀYIN, or UDAYĀŚVA, or UDAYANA, grandson of AJĀTAŚATRU, according to the *Vāyu Purāṇa* (WILSON, 467) and *Sutta piṭaka*.

Valley, and one of the hilly fastnesses to which the vigorous invading Aryans fondly clung, and transferred his seat of government out to the new city in the centre of the plain. Thus when the conquest of all the adjoining and upper provinces welded India for the first time into one great dominion, *Pāṭaliputra* became the capital of that vast empire.

It is at this period, about 300—302 B.C., that we first get a trustworthy account of the city. This is from the pen of the Greek ambassador, and it is unique in supplying the first fixed date for ancient India by the contemporary references through Greek history. In this first authentic glimpse into ancient India, it is remarkable that the influence of the Greeks should be so manifest at its capital.

The then reigning king, CHANDRA-GUPTA, or '*Sandrakottos*,' as the Greeks called him,[1] had, it seems, early come into intimate contact with the Greeks and into immediate relations with ALEXANDER-THE-GREAT in the Panjāb, during the latter's invasion of Northern India in 326 B.C. According to the historians of the Macedonian,[2] "this prince was of humble origin, but was called to royalty by the power of the gods; for having offended ALEXANDER by his impertinent language he was ordered to be put to death and escaped only by flight . . . . . . and collecting bands of robbers he roused the Indians to renew the empire. In the wars which he waged with the captains of ALEXANDER he was distinguished in the van mounted on an elephant of great size and strength. Having thus acquired power, SANDRAKOTTOS reigned at the same time that SELEUKOS laid the foundation of his dominion."[3] And Buddhist tradition places the original home of his family, the *Mora* or *Mayūra* (known to the Brahmans as '*Maurya*') on the slopes of the Himalayas

[1] The identity of the '*Sandrakottos*' of the Greeks with CHANDRA-GUPTA was first shown by Sir W. JONES, *Asiatick Researches*, IV, 11 (1795); and WILFORD noticed (*As. Res.*, V, 262) that the form used by ATHENÆUS was even closer, namely, '*Sandrakoptus*.' The '*Androkottos*' of PLUTARCH is also this same person.

[2] As noted in PLUTARCH'S *Life of Alexander* under name of '*Androkottus*,' also next note.

[3] JUSTIN, XV, 4.

in Northern India;[1] whilst another legend associates the *Mayūra rāja* and a *stūpa*-building prince of the *Sākya* race with the country over the *Mora* pass in the *Swāt* Valley,[2] whence I secured for the Indian Museum many Buddhist sculptures,[3] nearly all of which curiously bear the '*Mora*' symbol (a peacock); and certainly in this region, as these sculptures show, Greek influence was predominant two or three centuries later. In keeping also with this alleged northern origin of CHANDRA-GUPTA are the Brahmanical accounts, which refer to him as an outsider who with the aid of 'armed bands of robbers' and associated with the *Yavanas* (or Westerns) overran and conquered India.[4]

The Greek account of him and of the military despotism which he established thus pithily describes his relations with SELEUKOS NIKATOR, the immediate successor of ALEXANDER:—

"SELEUKOS NIKATOR . . . . . . first seizing *Babylon*, then reducing *Baktrianē*, his power being increased by the first success: thereafter he passed into India, which since ALEXANDER'S death killed its governors, thinking thereby to shake off from its neck the yoke of slavery. SANDRAKOTTOS (*i.e.*, CHANDRA-GUPTA) had made it free, but when victory was gained, he changed the name of freedom to that of bondage, for he himself oppressed with servitude the very people which he had rescued from foreign dominion. SANDRAKOTTOS having thus gained the crown held India at the time when SELEUKOS was laying the foundations of his future greatness. SELEUKOS . . . . . . waged war on SANDRAKOTTOS[5] . . . . . . "until he made friends and entered into relations of marriage with him,"[6] and "receiving in return five

[1] *Mahāvaṁso*, Turnour, Introd. XXXIX. Two of the rail-bars of the Bharhut *stūpa* dating almost to Asoka's epoch are inscribed as the gifts of THUPADĀSA and "GHATILA's mother," both of '*Mora*' hill. [2] *Hiuen Tsiang's Records* (BEAL) I, 126.

[3] *Actes du Onzième Congrès Internat. des Orientalistes*, Paris, 1897, Sect. I, p. 245. See also *Asiatic Quarterly Review* (October 1895).

[4] See footnote, p. 6.

[5] JUSTINUS, XV, 4. This must have been in 313 B.C., as SELEUKOS returned to Babylon in 312 B.C., thus giving CHANDRA-GUPTA's accession as about 315 or 316 B.C., which is the first fixed date for Indian history. *Cf.* also DR. HŒRNLE's note in *Centenary Rept.* As. Socy. (Beng.), 87.

[6] APPIANUS (*Syriake*, c. 55).

hundred elephants"[1] "and settling affairs on this side of India directed his march against ANTIGONUS."[2]

SELEUKOS sent his personal friend MEGASTHENES as ambassador to CHANDRA-GUPTA'S court at *Pāṭaliputra*. That historian describes the city[3] as being about 9 miles in length. It was surrounded by a wooden wall, pierced by many towered gateways, and with numerous openings in front for the discharge of arrows, and in front a ditch for defence and as a city sewer. It had a population of about 400,000, and the retinue of the king numbered many thousands. It is remarkable that in describing in considerable detail the religion of the people he makes no reference to Buddhism,[4] although Buddha had died about a century before; and the Sanskritic way in which he spells the proper names, especially in the retention of the letter *r*, seems to show that the *Pāli* form of dialect was not in use, and presumably was later in origin, although it is customary to represent Buddha as speaking always in this dialect.

This intercourse with the Greeks appears to have been closely maintained, for it is recorded that the son of SANDRAKOTTOS, "AMITROCHATES (? *Amitroghāta*),[5] and 'SOPHAGA-SENAS'[6] reinforced the armies of ANTIOCHOS, the son of SELEUKOS, and of ANTIGONUS-THE-GREAT with elephants" in their wars with the Persians. The Greek account relates that this king of *Pāṭaliputra*, AMITROCHATES, wrote to ANTIOCHOS asking the latter to buy and send him sweet wine, dried figs and a sophist; and that ANTIOCHOS replied: "We shall send you the figs and the wine, but in Greece the laws forbid a sophist to be sold."[7]

[1] STRABO, Geog. XV, 724, Bohn's trans. [2] JUSTIN XV, 4.

[3] *Megasthenis Indica*, a critical collection of translations from the Greek and Latin fragments of Megasthenes' lost work by SCHWANBECK. Bonn, 1846, and partly translated into English by J. W. MCCRINDLE in his *Ancient India*, 1877 and 1893. MEGASTHENES died 291 B.C.

[4] The '*Sarmania*' clad in the bark of trees were clearly Brahmanist *Sramaṇa* ascetics as LASSEN recognised by *Indisch. Alt.*, ii, 700.

[5] STRABO gives this name as ALLITROCHADES—it was probably meant for the Sanskrit title *Amitra-ghāta* or 'Enemy-slayer.' *Cf.* WILFORD *As. Res.*, v, 286.

[6] If this be intended for *Subhaga-sena*, it also would be an official title and not a personal name.—LASSEN, *Ind. Alt.*, ii, 273.

[7] ATHENAIOS, XIV, 67.—*Ancient India*, ed. 1893, p. 409.

The pomp and chivalry, the intrigues at court and the battles fought around the strong fortifications of *Pāṭaliputra* in these early days are vividly pictured in an Indian drama, which, although only composed about the middle ages, seems to have been based on earlier books now lost.[1]

It was, however, as the splendid capital of the celebrated warrior-prince, ASOKA (about B.C. 250), the grandson of CHANDRAGUPTA, that it is most widely known. This greatest of Indian emperors, the Constantine of Buddhism, may almost be said to have made Buddhism a religion, that is to say, a real religion of the people. For previous to his day it seems to have been little more than a struggling order of mendicant monks, so few apparently in number about 300 B.C. that, as we have seen, the Greek historian does not even refer to them. When, however, ASOKA was converted to this faith in his later life he made it the state-religion, and of a more objective and less abstract character, so that it appealed to the people in general, and he actively propagated it by missionaries and otherwise even beyond his own dominions. He was one of the most lavish devotees the world has ever seen. He covered his mighty kingdom, from *Afghanistan* to *Mysore*, from *Nepal* to *Gujerat*, with stately Buddhist monuments and buildings of vast size, regardless of expense. With his truly imperial and artistic instincts, so clearly derived more or less directly from the Greeks and Assyrians, his monuments were of the stateliest kind. His stupendous *stūpas* or mounds of solid masonry to enshrine Buddha's relics or to mark some sacred spot are found all over India, and are almost like Egyptian pyramids in size. His colossal edict-pillars, single shafts of stone, thirty to forty feet in length and beautifully polished and sculptured, still excite the wonder and admiration of all who see them. How magnificent, then, must have been the capital of this great Indian monarch, who, as we learn from some of his stone-

[1] The *Mudrā Rākshasa*, translated by Dr. H. H. WILSON, of the Indian Medical Service, in his *Hindu Theatre*.

cut edicts in the remoter parts of his empire, was the ally of the Greek kings ANTIOCHUS II of Syria, PTOLEMY of Egypt, ANTIGONOS GONATUS of Macedon, MAGAS of Cyrene, and ALEXANDER of Epirus, and how important for historical purposes are likely to be his edicts and other inscriptions in his own capital, which were seen there in the early part of our era, and are now in all probability buried in the ruins of the old metropolis.

The buildings previous to his epoch, as well as the walls of the city, seem all to have been of wood, like most of the palaces, temples and stockades of Burma and Japan in the present day. The change which he effected to hewn stone[1] was so sudden and impressive and the stones which he used were so colossal that he came latterly to be associated in popular tales with the giants or genii (*yaksha*)[2] by whose superhuman agency it was alleged he had reared his monuments; and a fabulous romantic origin was invented for his marvellous capital.[3]

It was possibly owing to ASOKA's gigantic stone buildings that the Greeks ascribed the building of the city to Hercules, for they had several accounts of it subsequent to the time of MEGASTHENES.[4] It is also possible that this legend of the giants may have partly arisen through ASOKA having made use of sculptured figures of the giants to adorn his buildings. The two colossal statues of these 'builders' of his monuments, now in the Indian Museum, were unearthed in his capital, and bear their names inscribed in characters only a little later than his epoch.[5] The stone out of which they are carved is identical

---

[1] *See* Appendix I.

[2] The *Asoka-avadāna*, BURNOUF's *Introd à l'Hist. du Buddhisme Indien*, 373.

[3] Appendix II.

[4] DIODÔRUS, writing in the 1st Century B. C., bases part of his account on the narrative of JAMBULUS, who after being seven years in Ceylon was wrecked "upon the Sandy shallows of India and forthwith carried away to the King, then at the city of '*Polybothia*,' many days' journey from the sea, where he was kindly received by the King who has a great love for the Grecians. * * * This JAMBULUS committed all these adventures to writing."—*Sic. Hist.* I, II, c. 4.

[5] Appendix III.

with that of his pillars, and they exhibit the same high polish which is found on few Indian sculptures of a subsequent era.

The influence of the West upon the Indian art of his time is especially conspicuous in the classic Assyrian and Greek conventional designs sculptured on his pillars; for example, the anthemion and honeysuckle friezes on the capitals. Indeed, this fact, coupled with the excellence of the workmanship, although these are the very first examples of stone sculpture found in India, leads to the probability that he employed Greek or Syrian artists in this work. Personally too he is said by a *quasi*-historic Buddhist legend[1] to have been governor for some years of *Taxila*—that old city of the Panjab, three marches east of the Indus, where Greek influence was strongly established at ALEXANDER's day.

But before the dawn of our era the great city *Pāṭaliputra* had decayed with the downfall of ASOKA's dynasty and the transfer of the capital elsewhere, and the influence doubtless of some of the three 'perils' predicted for it—'fire, water, and internal strife'— for such purported prophecies often embody historical facts, recorded after the events have happened; and this might easily be the case in the present instance, as the earliest date for the very earliest extant Buddhist scripture is only about 24 B.C.[2]

Its position peculiarly exposed it to destruction by water. The fickle rivers, which called it into being, are ever shifting their channels in their oscillations through the broad plain. At one time caressing the banks, at another they tear the latter furiously to

[1] *Asoka-avadāna* and the Tibetan *Vinaya*, III, 92, state that 'JIVAKA,' a natural son of BIMBASĀRA (that is, about five generations before ASOKA) went from Rājgir to Taxila to study medicine.

[2] This is usually given as 88—76 B.C. by MAX MÜLLER and others, calculating from the Ceylonese data supplied by TURNOUR; but TURNOUR in his table (*Mahāwamso*, p. lx) gives the date on which the scriptures were first reduced to writing in Ceylon as 218 years after Buddhism was introduced into that country by Asoka's mission. This mission, he shows, was sent in the 17th year of Asoka's reign. Now Asoka's reign is usually taken as beginning about 260 B.C., and the mission must have taken the greater part of the year to reach Ceylon. Thus we get the date 24 B.C. for the first manuscript copy of the Buddhist scriptures in Ceylon, and this is the source of the very earliest Pāli versions now extant.

pieces, and then desert the place for many miles. Plague also may have played some part in the ruin of the old capital, as it seems to have done at *Gaur* and other of the later 'dead cities' of the Ganges during the middle ages. Glimmerings of internal strife tempting foreign devastation seem to be had in the invasions from the south and by Scythians from the north about the beginning of our era.

In the third to the fifth centuries A.D. it seems to have been, for a time at least, the capital of the Imperial Gupta dynasty, several members of which patronised Buddhism.[1] In the fifth century, the Chinese Buddhist pilgrim, FA HIAN, found it still a large town with many of ASOKA's buildings in good preservation, and he gives a glowing account of their marvellously "elegant carving and inlaid sculpture work."[2] It was still a seat of Buddhist learning with 'six or seven hundred monks,' and he resided there for three years, copying rare scriptures which he had searched for in vain in Upper India.

The next two centuries witnessed a rapid change for the worse. The Chinese pilgrim HIUEN TSIANG about 635 A.D. found the city and its buildings a mass of crumbling ruins and "long deserted;"[3] though he notes that the monasteries, Hindu temples and "*stūpas*, which lie in ruins, may be counted by hundreds. There are only two or three remaining entire."[4] These latter also would seem even to have fallen into ruins, and on the extinction of Buddhism in India by the Muhammadan invasion in the twelfth century, even the very site and name of the city seem to have been generally forgotten.

Thus, when European enquirers towards the end of the eighteenth century began unearthing the lost history of India,

[1] The true date of these Guptas was discovered by PRINSEP *Jour. Asiatic Socy.* (Beng.), III, 115; VII, 975, 679, and has since been established by FLEET and others. They were of the 'Lunar' race (the *Mauryas* were of the 'Solar'), and latterly changed the capital from *Pāṭaliputra* to *Kanauj* (PRINSEP *l. c.*, III, 116).

[2] LEGGE's Travels of Fa Hien, p. 77. Appendix IV.

[3] See Appendix IV.

[4] *Idem*

none even of the most learned natives could give any clue to its whereabouts. In this state of uncertainty many conflicting conjectures were hazarded as to its location.

This lost city of the Ganges was supposed by some, from the meagre Greek accounts,[1] to be at such widely distant places as *Allahabad*,[2] *Rājmahal* near the junction of the *Kusi* River,[3] *Bhagalpur*,[4] and elsewhere. Its true position seems first to have been indicated in a general way by Major RENNELL about 1783,[5] as being near the modern *Patna;* and DR. BUCHANAN-HAMILTON, of the Indian Medical Service, in his admirable survey of *Patna* about 1808 ascertained that the local priests of the place retained the oral tradition that the ancient name of the place was '*Pāṭaliputra*,' though they could give no material proof for this, and even with their aid he failed to find any physical trace of that ancient city[6] after diligent search. This position for it was confirmed by the discovery in China of those remarkably detailed itineraries of the two Chinese Buddhist monks above mentioned, who in their pilgrimages had visited the town in the fifth and seventh centuries A.D., and had left descriptions of the chief sites in it and its neighbourhood.

The geographical details supplied by these narratives[7] clearly showed that the lost city must have been situated at or near *Pātna;*[8] and a local survey of the topography of that neighbourhood disclosed the fact that the river *Sōn* had formerly joined the Ganges there, and Mr. RAVENSHAW[9] believed that the mounds of

[1] MEGASTHENES in his itinerary placed it at 475 miles down the Ganges from its junction with the *Jamuna* (*i.e.*, at Allahabad) and 635 miles (6,000 *stadia*) from the mouth of the Ganges—PLINY as analysed by M. V. de St. MARTIN in *Étude sur le Geographie Grecque, &c.*, 132.

[2] D'ANVILLE—*vide* V. de St. MARTIN, *op. cit.*

[3] WILFORD, *Asiatick Researches*, V (1798) and XIV, 380 (1822).

[4] W. FRANCKLIN, Inquiry Concerning the Site of the Ancient Palibothra: London, 1815.

[5] *Memoir of a Map of Hindustan*, 1783.

[6] *Eastern India* I, 87.

[7] Translated into English and French by JULIEN, KLAPROTH, BEAL, and others.

[8] V. St. MARTIN *op. cit.* and in JULIEN'S '*Memoires*,' 1857, III, 372.

[9] *Jour. Asiatic Soc.* (Beng.) (1845), XIV, 137.

*Pānch-Pahāri* were the ruined bastions of the old city, of which last, however, he could find no trace. Then the staff of the Archæological Survey reported as the result of their search for it that "Modern Patna consequently does not stand on the site of old Pāṭaliputra, but very close to it, the *old city having occupied what is now the bed of the Ganges* and perhaps part of the great islands between Patna and Hajipur, on the opposite side of the river. *All or almost all traces of the ancient city must long since have been swept away by the Ganges.*"[1] Latterly, in 1878, the director of the archæological survey, General CUNNINGHAM himself, to whose unique knowledge of Indian antiquities we owe so much and who collected in his reports many references concerning *Pātaliputra*, expressed his belief, as a result of his subsequent visits to *Patna*, that remains of the old city still existed at *Chhoti* and *Pānch Pahāri*, to the south of the railway; and within the manifestly too narrow limits of these mounds he thrust all ASOKA's palaces, the monuments and monasteries of the great city.[2] The general opinion, however, prevalent amongst the local officers and other residents, who had deliberately searched for it, was that the site of the old city had been entirely washed away by the Ganges, and that not a trace of it remained.

It was at this stage that I, impressed with the importance of recovering, if possible, for science and the history of civilization, some of the monuments and records of this great lost city, took advantage of a hurried visit to *Patna* in 1892 to satisfy myself as to the real state of matters. On exploring the place I was surprised to find that not only was the ancient site practically unencroached on by the Ganges, but that most of the leading landmarks of ASOKA's palaces, monasteries, and other monuments remained so very obvious that I was able in the short space of one day to identify many of them beyond all doubt, by taking the itineraries of the Chinese pilgrims as my guide.

[1] "Archæological Survey of India" *Report*, VIII, 24, 1878.
[2] *Idem—Reports* XI, 151—160 (1881), and XV, pp. 1—3 (1882).

These itineraries of devoted Chinese Buddhist monks, FA HIAN, HIUEN TSIANG, and others, which were originally intended as guide-books to their fellow-countrymen in visiting the various sacred Buddhist spots, have afforded us the chief clue to recovering the ancient geography of India. Although they were written by simple pilgrims unprovided with a compass, their descriptions, distances, and directions have generally turned out to be marvellously trustworthy. Personally, after having tracked these itineraries for many hundreds of miles in the adjoining and other parts of India, I had come to place much trust in their general accuracy.

On piecing together, then, these Chinese topographical accounts of *Pāṭaliputra* (the texts of which are herewith attached for reference, as Appendix IV), and on projecting the details upon paper, we get the annexed rough plan of the great capital.

From it we see that all the chief monuments and palaces lay to the south of the old city, which itself fringed the right bank of the Ganges. It also is evident that the area of the chief monuments was bounded on the north and on the south by two great artificial mounds "like little mountains." The most northerly of these artificial hills was the hermitage "mountain" raised by ASOKA for his young and sole surviving brother, Prince MAHENDRA, who had become a Buddhist recluse and dwelt in BUDDHA's old cave in the "Vulture's Peak" in the far off hills of *Rājgir*. ASOKA in order to keep his brother near him built for him, with gigantic stones, as reported in the pilgrim's accounts, an artificial hill with a cell in a 'solitude' to the north of and near the palace. The most southerly of these great mounds was that formed by the clustered ruins of the five great *stūpas* which ASOKA built to enshrine BUDDHA's relics, and which HIUEN TSIANG described as "lofty . . . . . . at a distance they look like little hills."

The first spot, therefore, to which I hastened on my first visit to *Patna* was the most northerly of the large mounds in that

PLAN I.

# Location of Monuments according to Chinese descriptions.

(To face page 12.)

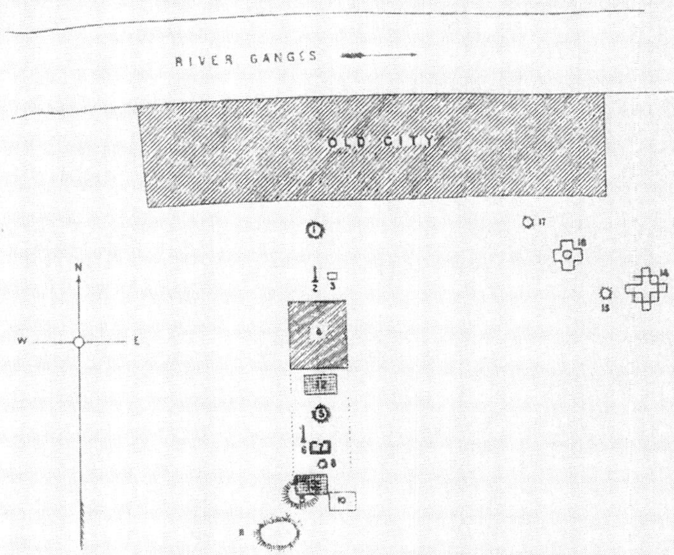


1 Prince Mahendra's Hermitage Hill
2 'Nili-' or Hell-Pillar
3 Alms-Trough
4 'Old Palace'
5 Great Relic-*Stupa*
6 World-Gift Pillar
7 Foot-Print Stone and Temple
8 Previous Buddha's Sitting Place
9 Upagupta's Hermitage Hill
10 Sacred Pond
11 Residuary Relic-*Stupas*
12, 13 Monasteries
14 Cock Monastery (*Kukkutarama*)
15 Amla-Fruit Offering *Stupa*
16 *Stupa* in Gong Monastery
17 Site of 'Devil-Inspired' Heretic.

L. A. WADDELL.

town, especially as it bore the highly suggestive title of 'the hill of the Buddhist mendicant monk,' namely, '*Bhikna Pahāri.*'

This 'hill' I found to be an artificial mound about twenty feet high and about a quarter of a mile in circuit, but consisting apparently of brick ruins, not stone, although three large blocks of stone, nearly a cubic yard each, lay on the surface, about a hundred yards to the north-east, and other large stones near its eastern base. But the most curious thing which I found was that a rude image which stood on the top of the great mound is called 'The mendicant Prince' (*Bhikna Kuṅwār*).

This image is over six feet high, and differs from the ordinary conical mound-idols of India not only in its great size, but also in that it has the shape of an elongated hillock deeply scooped out on its southern face to form two masses—a larger and smaller—with a deeper recess between them near the centre, from which latter point a track runs obliquely down to the bottom. The whole contour conveys the impression of a two-peaked hill with a path running up obliquely from the left to a cell between the two peaks, and it recalled to my mind the topography of the identical cave where Prince MAHENDRA had lived in the *Rājgir* hills, namely, the cave of the "Vulture's Peak" in the *Rājgir* hills. Indeed, it seemed as if not only did the tradition of the Prince's artificial hill still cling to this mound, but the Prince himself under the form of his hermitage was still actively worshipped by the people of *Patna*, in the same way as their ancestors in the Buddhist period must have worshipped or reverenced the actual hill and its princely recluse in ASOKA's day.[1] This would be a remarkable fact in the history of image-worship if it proved true—namely, that the leading topographical features of the hill have been retained in a mud model after so many centuries, notwithstanding that its mud requires frequent repair, and its present-day worshippers do not recognise that their image represents a hill at all; though this latter consideration counts for very little, as we know the tendency in Indian worship

[1] The offerings made in front are milk, rice, flowers and silk-thread.

to blindly perpetuate a form or rite mechanically once it has become stereotyped.

Be this as it may, the important fact remained that I found here, to the north of the other great mounds at *Pātna*, an artificial 'hill' with some huge blocks of stone near its base, retaining in its names vestiges of the Buddhist period; and the names themselves denoting 'the hill of the Buddhist Mendicant' and 'the Mendicant Prince;' *the* historical mendicant prince of *Pāṭaliputra* having been, as we have seen, ASOKA's brother, Prince MAHENDRA, whose artificial hermitage 'hill' lay to the north of all the other great monuments of ASOKA.

From here I made my way, as straight as possible, to the great mound on the south of *Pātna*, bearing the highly suggestive title of 'the five hills' (*Pānch Pahāri*, see map also plan II), as it will be remembered that the most southerly of all the monuments of the ancient city was the group of the five great *stūpas* of ASOKA, the ruins of which were described in the seventh century as being like 'little hills;' and I found that they by their position, form, and traditions were without doubt the ruins of these very identical five '*stūpas*.'

In this way, having fixed beyond doubt the fact that the most southerly mass of ruins of ASOKA's capital still existed in much the same condition as in HIUEN TSIANG's day, and that the tradition of a mendicant prince still lingered in the neighbourhood of the most northerly of the extant mounds about two miles distant, and the intervening area, I saw, contained numerous mounds, with several sculptured slabs of ASOKA's epoch lying about, under trees, or at wells, or plastered into the walls of buildings, it was clear that the chief sites within the limits of the old city were still practically intact, and had not been washed away by the Ganges or other river, as generally supposed, and that many structural remains of ASOKA's city still existed. And as positive proof that this was indeed the old city, I discovered within the *Jain* temple (21 on map) an inscription (see plate VII) giving '*Pāḍali-pura*' as the name of the place.[1] This seems the first occasion on which the actual ancient name had been found at or near *Pātna*.

Next day, I found that *portions of the old wooden walls of the city as described by Megasthenes still existed* in this area[2] actually *in situ!* The great beams are found buried fifteen to twenty feet below the present surface level, when the villagers dig wells in particular places. On striking these great beams standing erect so many feet below the surface, the superstitious villagers, unable to account for the presence of the huge posts, usually abandon their attempted wells. But although the local tradition has thus been lost, I noticed the curious fact that the caste which occupies the small wards adjoining these old wooden walls are almost exclusively the Bow-men ('*Dhānuk*'), probably the descendants of the old soldiery who kept watch and ward over these battlements in ancient times!

I also by a hurried inspection of several of the mounds and villages found various fragments of sculptures and other confirmatory details which led me to conclude that the modern village of *Kumrāhar* (17 on map) covered the site of the greater part of the old palace, the remains of which latter were deeply buried twelve to twenty feet below the surface; and that the ruins of others of the ancient buildings existed at the various spots numbered on the accompanying map. As to the identity of some of these, I hazarded a few provisional conjectures, but I expressly added, "the real nature of most of these mounds can only be revealed by actual excavation." At the same time, I pointed out that the necessary exploratory excavation must inevitably be very difficult and costly owing to the fact that most of the likely sites are largely built over or covered by Muhammadan graves, and because the old ruins lie deeply buried down in the *debris* of over twenty centuries, often with little or no surface-marking to indicate their presence.

[1] *Pāḍali* is the current Hindi form for the name of the flower '*Pāṭali*;' the *ṭ* is replaced by *ḍ*. For further details see Appendix IX, p. 83.

[2] The existence of some beams several miles away within the city of Patna had been recorded by Mr. McCRINDLE in 1877—see p. 21.

These important results of my hurried two days' visit I reported at once to the Government of Bengal, who forthwith printed and published my rough notes on the subject.[1] The great interest thus excited amongst European orientalists by the discovery that the exact site of ASOKA's classic capital was still extant, and contained structural remains and probably invaluable historical inscriptions earlier than any hitherto known, led to an influential request being addressed to Government to make the necessary excavations at the spots indicated by me.

To this, Government generously assented, and granted funds for the work. Unfortunately, however, these primary excavations, begun in 1894, when I was absent on sick leave, were misdirected. They nevertheless confirmed my identification of the *Pānch Pahāri* as being the ruins of great *stūpas*, and also the already known fact that at the *Chhoti Pahāri* was a great *stūpa*,[2] which from my later inspection in 1892 I was inclined to think might be *the* celebrated first and greatest of all the relic-*stūpas* erected by ASOKA, as General CUNNINGHAM had latterly supposed.

In 1895 Government asked me to direct and supervise the excavations which they wished to be made at the sites which I had indicated as lying within 'the old palace,' that is, the palace of the kings of the *Maurya* dynasty. Such excavations can only be done during the dry season, as it is only then that the level of the ground-water at most of the sites falls sufficiently to allow of the necessary deep digging. On visiting *Patna* for this purpose, I secured for the Calcutta museum all the various portions of Buddhist railings and other important pieces of sculptures which were lying about or fixed in buildings in accessible positions, after I had gained the consent of their owners. I was fortunate also in obtaining for the local supervision of the proposed excavations, as I could not be present personally, the active assistance of

[1] *Discovery of the exact site of Pāṭaliputra and description of the superficial remains*, 1892.

[2] CUNNINGHAM *Arch. S. Rept.*, XI, 158.

COLOSSAL CAPITAL QUASI-PERSEPOLITAN

Reduced to $\frac{1}{12}$th

Photo by L. A. Waddell.

Photogravure, Survey of India Offices, Calcutta, April 1903.

Mr. C. A. MILLS, of the Public Works Department, who was then stationed at *Patna*.

In May 1896 the exploratory trenches were commenced at the various spots pointed out by me at *Kumrāhar*, *Bulandhi*, *Bahadurpur*, and *Rampur*. Within a few days so many important sculptures and other objects were unearthed that I was telegraphed for to visit the excavations and advise further proceedings.

Mr. MILLS' telegram dated 22nd May 1896 was:—

"Have found stone carvings, beams, one coin supposed to be Chinese, images, foundation of buildings, moulded bricks, stone pebbles, etc. Please come by Saturday's mail if possible, as your advice as to further excavation is urgently needed."

These sculptures, on inspection, I found included the *magnificent colossal capital of a distinctly Greek type*—quasi-Ionic, figured in plate II. It was found twelve feet below the surface, on digging at a spot indicated by me in the *Bulandhi* grove of *mango* trees, where there was no surface-marking to guide me except a large rough stone with a peculiar legend attached to it like that related by HIUEN TSIANG in regard to Buddha's foot-print stone. This huge capital by its beautiful workmanship, material, and the depth at which it was found amongst ruined walls seemed manifestly of ASOKA's period or very soon after it. And the immense importance of this find is that *it is the most Grecian sculpture yet found in India*, excepting the capitals of ASOKA's pillars and the 'Indo-Grecian' statues and friezes of the Panjāb; and that *it is found within the palace precincts of* ASOKA'S *own capital, and is probably of* ASOKA'S *own age!*

The other 'finds' thus brought to light were portions of old brick walls ten to fifteen feet below the surface, also ancient wooden bridges and piers or '*ghats*' along the ancient moats. These remains afforded clues to further promising sites for exploratory trenches. And in one of these positions, which I had thus indicated, Mr. MILLS, assisted by his surveyor, AHMED HOSSAIN, had the rare good fortune in June 1896 to find (at 16 on map), about ten feet below the surface, the broken fragments of a gigantic pillar of ASOKA, one of those polished colossal monoliths which that emperor set up and inscribed with his ediots when no rocks were near, and of which two existed in his capital at the time it was visited by the Chinese pilgrims. Fragments of nearly half of the whole pillar were recovered, but these unfortunately bore no trace of the inscription. This missing portion or fragments of it will probably be found by further excavation near this place, for this seems to be the original situation of the pillar, because the exposed fragments lie in the centre of a court bordered by rows of monastic cells, built of massive bricks of the old Buddhist period. The expense, however, of the deep excavations necessary for this purpose is almost prohibitive.

The discovery of this pillar of ASOKA supplied another most important clue to the topography of the ancient palace and city. But this could not be followed up immediately, owing to the onset of the rainy season and the occurrence of famine in another part of the province withdrawing Mr. MILLS from this work. Ultimately about the beginning of 1897 a subordinate of the Public Works Department was sent to carry out my instructions, but he only very partially followed them, and so advanced the research very little.

In March last (1899) I was permitted by Government to visit *Patna* for a few days to report upon the whole question of the excavations there, and especially to show what had been achieved and what still remained to be done in the way of practicable excavation at the site of the old palace of ASOKA and the *Mauryas*. I went very carefully over the whole ground several times; and this in itself was no easy matter, as the old site extends over several square miles, and is thickly built over in great part, freely intersected with tortuous stretches of water—old channels of the river *Sōn*—and barred by groves and clumps of trees which cut off the view.

The result of this review of the situation, whilst confirming breadly and in most particulars my original identifications, as made at my two visits in 1892, extends considerably our knowledge of several important details, and especially so of the limits of the palace and the position of its chief monuments, as will be seen in the accompanying map, plans, and photographs.

In detailing these particulars I shall first consider the question as to the boundaries of the old city, then the extent and boundaries of the palace, and afterwards the sites of the chief individual monuments as far as can be ascertained at present.

## THE CITY OF PĀTALIPUTRA:

### ITS LOCATION AND BOUNDARIES.

The geographical position of the city is fixed, by the foregoing data, at a point somewhere in the immediate vicinity of the modern town of *Pātna*. The old city stood on the south bank of the Ganges at the confluence of the latter river with another, called by the Greeks '*Erranoboas*,' a name apparently intended for the river *Hiranyabahu* or *Sōn*,[1] which formerly joined the Ganges here, and in the accompanying map I have indicated in green the present traces of the old channel of the *Sōn*, which seems to be the river in question.

As the city was recorded to have lain more than half-a-mile[2] to the north of the palace, and as we have found vestiges of the palace at the village of *Kumrāhar* (see map), I thus began my

[1] STRABO does not name this river, but ARRIAN, writing apparently from the same sources (MEGASTHENES), calls it '*Erranoboas*,' which is usually considered to be intended for the Indian '*Hiranya-baha*' or 'The Golden Armed,' a title which Sir W. JONES showed [*Asiatic Researches*, IV, 10 (1796)] was an ancient name of the river Son, and Colonel WILFORD (*idem*, XIV, 380) quotes PATANJALI as writing 'Pāṭaliputra on the Son' (*anu Sonam Pāṭaliputra*) also Ind. Antiquary, 1872, p. 201). But ARRIAN and PLINY enumerate both the '*Erranoboas*' and '*Son*' as distinct rivers. It might also be intended for the *Hiranyavati* or The 'Golden One,' which was a title of the *Gandak* or one of its branches at the time and place where Buddha died; and the *Gandak* joins the Ganges opposite *Patna* at the present day.

[2] 'More than three *li* to the south of this city' was the great relic-*stupa* which was '*within* the royal precincts.' FA HIAN—See Appendix IV

search for the boundaries of the old city to the north of that village.

The form of the city, about B.C. 300, we learn from MEGASTHENES, was a long parallelogram about nine miles in length, apparently fronting the Ganges. His description is as follows:—

"At the meeting of this river (the Ganges) with another is situated '*Palibothra*,' a city eighty *stadia* (9·2 miles) in length and fifteen (1·7 miles) in breadth. It is of the shape of a parallelogram and is girded with a wooden wall, pierced with loopholes for the discharge of arrows. It has a ditch in front for defence and for receiving the sewage of the city.[1] This ditch which 'encompassed it (the city) all round' was six hundred feet in breadth and thirty cubits in depth, and the wall was crowned with 570 towers and had four-and-sixty gates."[2]

In the seventh century A.D. the ruins of ASOKA's city were still 12 to 14 miles[3] "in circuit: although it is waste and desolate, the parapets of the walls still remain."[4]

Such a long strip of high-lying and densely-inhabited land we still find in the direction and general position here indicated, namely, about half-a-mile to the north of the village of *Kumrāhar* which latter is a part of the old palace. It stretches from *Bankipur* on the west to beyond *Pātna* city on the east, about eight miles in length, and it is bounded on three sides by deep moats and on the fourth or north side by the Ganges. The 'moat' on the south side, averaging about 200 yards in width and still retaining water for the greater part of the year, is an old channel of the *Sōn*, the same which had been utilized in its eastern portion by the Muhammadans as the southern moat to their fortifications at *Pātna* (see map). On the west are several moats representing probably reductions in the size of the city by encroachments of the river or otherwise.

[1] STRABO, XV, i, 35-36; McCrindle's *A.I.*, 67.
[2] ARRIAN *Indica* 10; McCrindle, 68.
[3] "About seventy *li*," HIUEN TSIANG's *Life* (Beal), p. 101.
[4] *Idem*, 101.

Within the oblong tract thus demarcated, *Patna* 'city' seems without doubt to occupy part of the site of the ancient *Pāṭaliputra*, and at its high south-west corner stood, in my opinion, the village of *Pāṭali* ('*Pāṭali-grāma*') which formed the nucleus of the ancient city. The popular shrine of the 'city-goddess' (*Pātan Devi*) further to the west doubtless also stands on part of the old city, together with the higher lying ground by *Bhikna Pahāri* towards *Bankipur*. The western border of the city cannot, however, be defined at present, even approximately, owing to the land there having been so much cut up by the swirl of the Ganges and *Sōn* rivers. Nor can the eastern limit be indicated with certainty; for the line of beam-palisades discovered at the place marked (* *) on the map does not show whether it defined the extreme eastern border of the city or merely bounded an arm of the moat.

In attempting to trace and map out the boundaries of the old city, our most trustworthy, guide, in the absence of superficial walls, or their indications, would obviously be the lines of this old buried beam-palisade, if we could find them. The first notice of the fact that vestiges of these old walls still exist was recorded in 1877.[1] They were found in the heart of the modern town of *Pātna* at the point above mentioned and here detailed:—

"During the cold season 1876 whilst digging a tank[2] in *Sheikh Mithia Ghari*, a part of Patna almost equally distant from the *chauk* (market-place) and the railway station, the excavators, at a depth of some 12 or 15 feet below the swampy surface, discovered the remains of a long brick wall running from north-west to south-east. How far this wall extended beyond the limits of the excavation—(which latter was) probably more than a hundred yards—it is impossible to say. Not far from the wall and almost parallel to it was found a line of palisades, the strong timber of which it was composed inclined slightly towards the wall. In one place there appeared to have been some sort of outlet for two wooden pillars rising to a height of some 8 or 9 feet above what had evidently been the ancient level of the place and between which no trace of palisade could be discovered, had all the appearance of door or gate-posts."

[1] J. W. McCrindle, *Ancient India as described by Megasthenes*, p. 207.
[2] Now called '*Mangle Sahib's talao.*'

Further traces of these old wooden walls were found by me in 1892 at several places, one to three miles distant, and in every case the tops of the beams were over 18 feet below the present level of the ground. The first of these is at the spot marked *19 on the map. This point is about 200 yards to the north of the sacred well called '*Āgam kuań*' and near the western border of the village *Tulsi Mandi*, by the side of a moat which is called by the older villagers 'The Emperor's Moat' (*Mahārāj khanda*). Here a cluster of about twenty-five to thirty beams were exposed in digging a tank about thirty years ago, and they remained visible for several years: some were carried off for firewood. I saw a portion of one of the beams and found it to be *sal* tree[1] about two feet in diameter, and though dark in colour marvellously well preserved. I also found that by the side of these beams the villagers had recently exposed the top of a heap of large, roughly splintered stones, each about two feet in diameter, and piled as if to prevent the beams from becoming undermined by the water. This was probably the site of one of those numerous wooden towers mentioned by MEGASTHENES at an inlet (door or canal) leading into the town from the south, or an outpost of the palace.

The two other points where I found portions of the beam-palisade still *in situ* are at *13 and *24 on map, of which particulars will be given presently with reference to the palace boundaries.

The structure of the palisade was probably similar to that figured in one of the friezes I obtained from the *Swat* valley, depicting the wooden fortifications of *Kapilavastu* and dating to about the 1st century of our era, when the traditional appearance of the old wooden walls had doubtless not been forgotten. In a portion afterwards traced[2] to the south of *Bulandhi*, the beams averaged 18 to 20 inches in diameter and appeared to be arranged in a double line, the one about 5½ feet distant from the other; and the individual posts seemed connected by

[1] *Shorea robusta.* | [2] By Babu Purnachandra.

transverse planks. The space between the double row of beams was probably filled with earth.

No further vestiges of the walls, wooden or brick, of the old city have yet been reported, though I have no doubt that any resident of *Bankipur* who kept an outlook on the wells, drains and tanks which are constantly being dug thereabouts would obtain many more.

Nevertheless from the general indications now available it seems fairly clear that relatively little of the ancient site has been cut away by the Ganges, probably less than half of the river frontage of the city. This river while habitually carrying away the land bodily for many miles in width to the north[1] appears to have spared the site of *Pāṭaliputrā* in great measure. It bends northward at *Bankipur*, which name indeed means 'the town of the (river-) bend.' It is curious, however, to find that the great fair of this part of Mid-India is held, not at *Patna*, but on the sands opposite to it, on the northern bank of the river at the confluence of the *Gandak*, which place curiously is called *Sonpur*. This, however, can scarcely refer to the river '*Sōn*,' as it is on the opposite side of the Ganges and is far from the ascertained site of the monuments of *Pāṭaliputra*.[2]

The greatest monuments of *Pāṭaliputra*, however, we are informed by the Chinese pilgrims, lay to the south of the city and chiefly within the Palace precincts.

[1] This is well illustrated in the following extract from a recent newspaper article on the encroachments of the river at Palasi opposite Patna:—

"The Ganges here will one day leave the landing ghat half-a-mile from the river, while a few days later it will cut the ghat and railway sidings away; another time a sand bank will suddenly appear in mid channel, and the authorities will have to find a new channel for their ferry steamer; that, perhaps, means a deviation of three or four miles, which makes a considerable difference in the time-table. This may remain open for a few weeks, and then gradually fill up again, and a new channel has to be found. This is Mother Ganges' oldest and most favourite amusement."

[2] Another name on the north bank which appears to me to possibly preserve one of the old names is that of the *ghat* or embarking place opposite the Bankipur end of Patna. The old name of this part of the country was according to the Greek account '*Prasi*,' which was interpreted by Surgeon Wilson, the great Sanskritist, as representing the Indian word '*Prāchya*, or 'Eastern, and this very probably is its real meaning. Still it seems worth noting that the opposite embarking place for Patna is called the ferry of '*Palasi*' or '*Parasi*.'

## THE PALACE.

The old palace, as containing within its grounds the chief ancient monuments, is therefore of more importance for us than the city itself. And we have the positive satisfaction of having found part of its ruins beyond all doubt.

It stood, according to the Chinese records, "to the south of the city,"[1] from which one of its chief monuments (the great *relic* stupa) was more than 3 *li*, that is, over half a mile. And the discovery of the broken *Asoka*-pillar and the position of the great *stupa* (28 on map) and the other sculptures and ruins of buildings disclosed by the excavations confirm my identification that *Kumrāhar* village covers a principal portion of the palace ruins. The tradition also of its villagers gives this place as the residence of the old *rāja* of the country, and especially of VIKRAMADITYA, who was one of the 'Imperial Guptas' kings of *Pāṭaliputra* about A.D. 400, and the oldest *rāja* of which they had heard.

What the size of the palace was is not stated either by the pilgrims or in any other published record that I can find. But to accommodate so many large monuments in addition to the retinue of such a mighty Eastern potentate and soldier as ASOKA was, it must have been of very large extent.

The 'camp' of SANDRAKOTTOS, as described by the Greek ambassador, contained 400,000 men. Of such a large army, only a fraction would likely be quartered in the palace or even in the city permanently; but its vast number conveys some idea of the large size of the palace itself. So also does the Greek description of life in the palace and the stately processions from it on business and pleasure, and the references to its large grounds and pleasure gardens.[2]

"The care of the King's person is entrusted to women, who also are bought from their parents. The guards and the rest of the soldiery attend outside the gates of the Royal apartments. The King may not

[1] See p. 72.

[2] One of the pleasure gardens within the Palace in ASOKA'S day is said (1) to have been named '*Rativaddhana*': *see Mahāvaṁso* Turnour, 41, also Appendix VII.

sleep during the daytime, and by night he is obliged to change his couch from time to time with a view to defeat plots against his life.[1]

"The King leaves his palace not only in time of war, but also for the purpose of judging causes. He then remains in court for the whole day. Another purpose for which he leaves his palace is to offer sacrifice; a third is to go to the chase, for which he departs in Bacchanalian fashion. Crowds of women surround him, and outside this circle spearmen are ranged. The road is marked off with ropes, and it is death for man and woman alike to pass within the ropes. Men with drums and gongs lead the procession . . . . . . Of the women, some are in chariots, some on horses, and some even on elephants, and they are equipped with weapons of every kind, as if they were going on a campaign."[2]

Although the precise boundaries of this great palace cannot yet be defined with any certainty, owing to the want of inscribed records *in situ*, and there being little on the surface to indicate the ruins underneath; still from the fact that we have found several fixed points (notably 'the five relic-*stupas* and the mounds of ruins' immediately to the north of these) and some of the actual monuments (the great stupa, portions of two old stone-railings, the *Asoka*-pillar, &c.) we may from these and the general topography provisionally consider that the palace stretched from *Chhoti Pahāri* (26 on map) to *Kumrāhar* with a north-western extension through *Bulandhi*, *Sandalpur*, *Bahadurpur*, even as far as *Pirthipur*, and that the ruins on which the '*Dargah*' (4 on map) now stands probably represents a detached northern portion of the palace on the way to the Ganges. This would give the Palace and its surrounding buildings and grounds an area of over four square miles, with a somewhat sinuous outline towards the south, bordering the old channels of the river *Sōn*. The line of very old ruined foundations which stretch almost continuously from *Chhoti Pahāri* to beyond *Bulandhi* shows that by ASOKA's time, whatever it may have been in Buddha's day, no large channel of the *Sōn* flowed in between.

[1] STRABO XV, i, 46—49: McC., 85.
[2] STRABO XV, i, 53—56: McC., 72.

In searching for traces of the boundaries of the old palace, I found what are evidently parts of its old wooden 'walls' or palisade in two or three localities. Firstly, north-west of *Kumrāhar* at the point (marked *2 on plan II) where in 1892 I had recorded one beam, further digging here exposed about sixteen feet below the surface, a line of several erect beams running east and west. The beams were of *sal* wood, about eighteen feet long by 14″×12″, and they evidently formed the northern boundary of a canal or old armlet of the *Sōn.* Again at *20 in plan II, about a quarter of a mile east of *Chhoti Pahāri*, in line with and due south of the clump of beams at *Tulsi Mandi* already referred to as forming part probably of the city walls, I found a similar group of enormous beams about eighteen feet below the surface.[1] The posts are clamped together with bands of iron. This seems to have been a pier or the foundation of a tower, and is on the western border of a very old site now called *Kharaunia*, where the *debris* of broken clay cooking vessels extends down for fifteen to twenty feet. Another erect beam was lately found on digging a well in the field close to the south-west corner of *Kumrāhar.* And at *Rampur* other beams were found which, however, seems more for drainage purposes than for defence.[2]

From the disposition of these beams and the topography of the country with reference to the *Sōn* channels, and the results of the excavations so far made, it would seem that the palace covered this large area to the south of the city, from which it was cut off by water-channels, of which smaller armlets seem to have penetrated the palace-grounds, and that both the palace and these water-channels were fortified by palisades. I have already noted the curious fact that the eastern border of this ancient stronghold is at the present day almost exclusively inhabited by the 'Bowmen'

[1] In a field belonging to Meghu Koiri.
[2] See after—p. 41.

caste, probably the descendants of the old palace guard of archers. I may also mention in this respect that these villagers have built on the outskirts of their hamlets special 'wrestling-grounds,' bricked and plastered platforms where the 'Bowmen' youth nowadays indulge in friendly rivalry their martial (?) instincts.

## Excavations on the Site of the Palace.

As the important ruins of these ancient times are so deeply buried in the dust and rubbish of subsequent centuries, it is necessary to resort to excavation in order to recover their vestiges. This operation reveals the interesting fact, as in digging into the older peat-mosses in Europe, that there is a chronological stratification, where each generation has left its own record.

This is especially evident in the fragments of pottery and bricks. On penetrating the thin superficial stratum of the present day with its fragments of bricks of the ordinary European proportions —as this standard employed by the Government Public Works Department is everywhere imitated by native builders, less than a foot brings us to the thin biscuit bricks of the Muhammadan period. On going further down we find the bricks become larger and larger during the earlier mediæval period, till at the depth of twelve to fifteen feet we reach those usually found in the buildings of Asoka's age, measuring sixteen to eighteen inches in length by ten to twelve in breadth and two to three inches in depth.

The rise in the general level of the country and of the beds of the rivers has been so great that many of the ancient buildings are covered now by open fields. Thus at *Kumrāhar* and around it most of the old buildings, monastic and other, are found deep beneath fields bearing crops of potatoes, pulse, and rice, and without practically any surface indications of their presence.

This rise in the surface level of the ground is partly due to the ruins of buildings, the accumulation of the refuse of villages, but mainly and chiefly to the silt deposited by the river floods, and also I think to a considerable extent to the dust caught and held fast by grass and weeds. The rate of this deposit as indicated by the depth at which the old remains are found would give about eighteen to twenty feet in about twenty-two centuries or less than one foot in a hundred years.[1] An interesting geological fact is that pebbles are found thus far out from the hills at a depth of about twenty feet.

But all this silting and covering up of the ancient surface tends to reduce the prominences and depressions in great measure to one dead level and effectually masks the ruins underneath, rendering their recovery a task of extreme difficulty. In this way one has to work almost entirely in the dark on the lines of a scientific research, and be ever on the alert to recognise clues when they present themselves and follow them up duly without destroying any structural vestiges. Besides this, the great depth to which the excavation must be carried to reach the ancient ground level takes much time and is very costly.

The first spot at which I commenced excavations was at *Kumrāhar* (11 on plan II), where that ancient pillar carved in deep relief had been found, inside the courtyard of the owner of that village, *Shaikh* AKRAM-UL-HAQ. This gentleman had obligingly presented to me for Government portions of a Buddhist railing and a few other sculptured stones which he or his ancestors had unearthed in digging wells or house foundations hereabout, and he at my request permitted his courtyard to be incised deeply in several directions. These trenches were carried down to over twelve feet by Mr. MILLS, but besides the fact that they showed that the whole thickness of that stratum was composed of broken bricks and plaster, which had frequently been dug over, they revealed no structural remain, except a winged *griffin* sculptured in white sandstone, 30 inches long.[2] It may be noted that griffins, although met with in Assyrian sculpture,

[1] A somewhat similar rate was also found in respect to the excavation of the old fort at Calcutta by Mr. C. R. WILSON. The remains of the previous century were found a little over one foot below the present surface level.

[2] Now in the Indian Museum.

## PLAN II.

# Actual Position of the Ruins.

(To face page 28.)

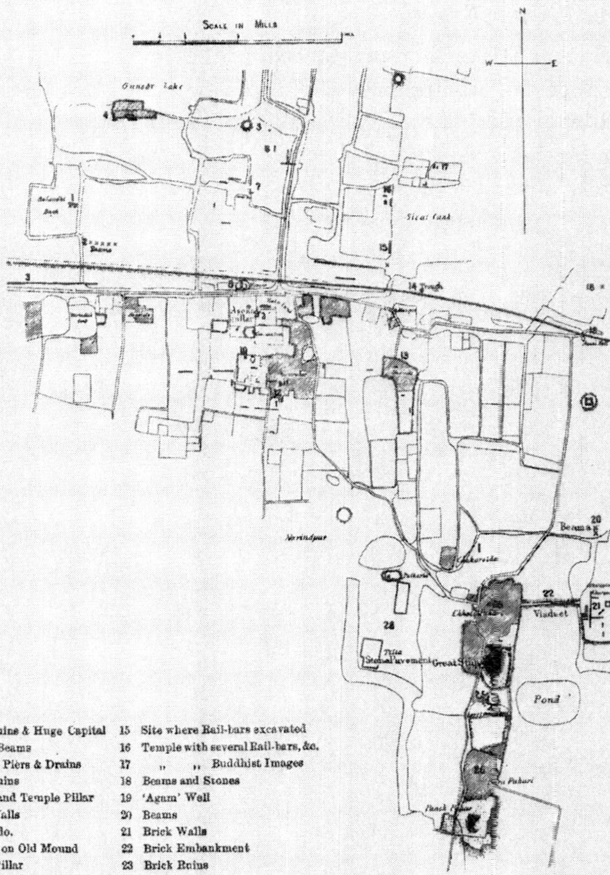


1 Brick Ruins & Huge Capital
2 Line of Beams
3 Wooden Piers & Drains
4 Brick Ruins
5 Mound and Temple Pillar
6 Brick Walls
7 Do. do.
8 Mosque on Old Mound
9 Asoka-Pillar
10 Rail Coping Stone
11 Land-Owner's House
12 Subterannean Passage
13 Brick Walls
14 Iron (?Stone) Trough
15 Site where Rail-bars excavated
16 Temple with several Rail-bars, &c.
17 " " Buddhist Images
18 Beams and Stones
19 'Agam' Well
20 Beams
21 Brick Walls
22 Brick Embankment
23 Brick Ruins
24 Great Stupa
25 High Brick Mound
26 Brick Ruins
27 The '5 Relic Stupas'
28 Stone Pavement.

L. A WADDELL.

are also specially referred to by the old Greek authors in their account of ancient India.[1]

The carved pillar which was unearthed here some years ago[2] bears on its two opposite sides the life-sized figure of a female in the old style, possibly of ASOKA's epoch, and resembling generally the reliefs with the giantesses (*Yakshini*) in the *Bharhut* railings.[3] Her uplifted hand grasps the branch of a tree bearing fruit somewhat like the jack-fruit,[4] and the sides are gracefully decorated with clusters of plantain[5] and *mango*[6] fruit.

A large wall was struck about twenty yards to the west of the court-yard (11, plan II), at six feet below the surface. It ran north and south, was 3½ feet thick, and its bricks were of the earlier mediæval kind, measuring 13″ × 10″ × 2″. Its foundation was reached at 8 feet below surface. It formed portion of a large building, possibly a *vihāra*, with a plastered brick pavement some yards further north, but nothing else noteworthy was found on carrying the trenches down to the mud-level. The whole site here consists of traces of brick foundations, which have been repeatedly dug into for bricks for building purposes; and on a little mound (at the point ×|10 on plan II) lies the coping stone of a Buddhist railing (plate I). This latter point is about a hundred yards south of the place where were found the fragments of the great *Asoka*-pillar, to be described presently.

---

[1] "Four-footed birds about as large as wolves, having legs and claws like those of the lion and covered all over the body with black feathers, except only on the breast, where they are red" (KTESIAS—McCrindle's transl., p. 17). Its beak is like an eagle's (*id.*, p. 44).

[2] It is now worshipped in the adjoining Hindu village of *Nayatola*.

[3] Especially the one inscribed *Chulakoka Devata* in CUNNINGHAM's "Stupa of Bharhut," pt. xxiii, 673. Were it not for the fact that a variety of such figures in various attitudes occur in the Bharhut sculptures and the fact that in this case both the left and right hands are uplifted on different sides, the figure by itself might be taken as intended for *Māya*—Buddha's mother in the conventional birth-scene.

[4] *Artocarpus integrifolia.* Major D. PRAIN, the Superintendent of the Botanic Garden, Calcutta, who has kindly examined the photograph, suggests that the tree may be intended for the Indian Screw-Pine (*Pandanus odoratissimus*, LINN.), although, as he remarks, the thorny character of the latter would prevent it being grasped as in the sculpture. This Screw-Pine, the fragrant *Ketaka*, or 'dust-flower,' *Dhuli-pushpika*, or *Gagan-dhul* is sacred to Vishnu and Krishna (*Pharmacographia Indica*, iii, 536).

[5] *Musa sapientum.* [6] *Mangifera Indica.*

South of the landlord's house, about thirty yards, I sank a well at the spot (12 on plan II), where according to a village tradition there was a subterranean masonry passage leading for several hundred yards in a north-westerly direction. After some difficulties, as the excavation at the spot originally pointed out showed no structure even at eighteen feet depth, I had to retire to allow the *zanana* women to be brought out to indicate the proper spot. This was reached by lateral mining, and a structure of large bricks was revealed twelve feet below the surface with a cavity partly faced which looked as if it might be a passage. But objections were raised to further undermining of the houses over it, so that it could not be ascertained whether there was an arch, and the interesting question of this subterranean passage remains unsolved. Although now so deeply buried, it was probably once a building above ground, and curiously, while the village legend says, the passage leads to the *Dargah*, about a mile to the north-west; there is also at the latter place a subterranean passage twenty feet below the surface, and also running north-west, in the direction of *Bhikna Pahari*.[1]

The most important find of all, perhaps, at these excavations at *Kumrāhar* was the discovery of a broken *Asoka*-pillar in the field at its north-west corner (9 plan II) between the *Chaman* and *Kalu* ponds, and adjoining the Grand Trunk Road and railway line. There was no surface indication here except that I noticed the villagers were digging out some large bricks (18″ × 11½″ × 2″), evidently of the Buddhist period, from rather superficial ruins bordering the south side of the latter pond; and in consequence I asked Mr. Mills to cut an exploratory trench across this high field. In doing this Surveyor Ahmad Hossain, who has rendered me much valuable and painstaking assistance throughout this enquiry, found on the 1st July 1896 a large fragment of a colossal *Asoka*-pillar twelve feet below the surface at the site marked B on annexed plan III. It was a vertical section of the shaft, three and-a-half feet long and nearly two and-a-half

[1] See p. 43 for further details of this *Dargah* passage.

PLAN III.

# Environs of Asoka Pillar.

(To face page 30.)

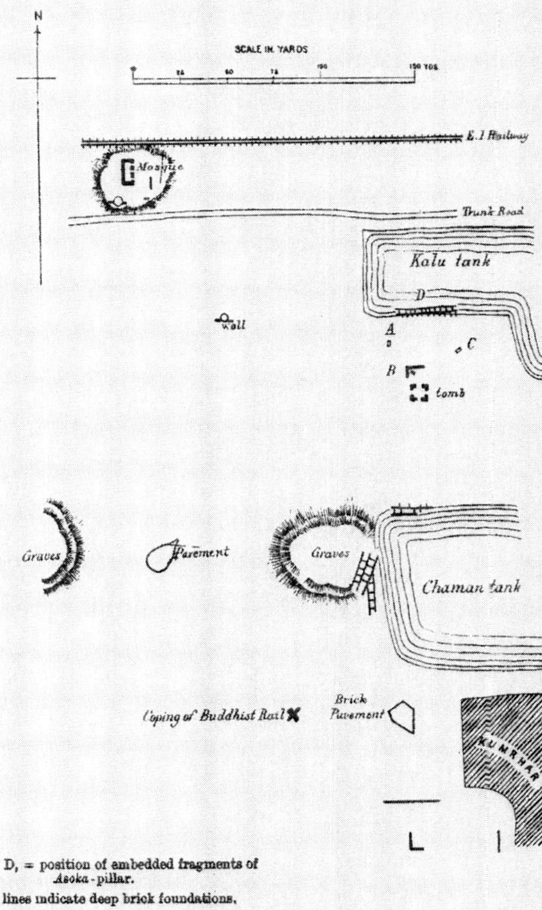


A, B, C, D, = position of ambedded fragments of *Asoka*-pillar.

The red lines indicate deep brick foundations.

L. A WADDELL.

feet in diameter, giving a circumference of about 7 feet 7 inches. It lay in the north-west corner of a rectangular wall built of the above-noted large bricks, and it rested on a stratum of broken pieces of bricks and mortar, together with numerous other splinters of its stone. The two walls enclosing it, which were struck ten feet below surface, also rested on the same foundation, so they evidently were built *after* the destruction of the pillar. Further digging exposed two other similar large fragments at the spots marked A and B on plan III, at ten and twelve feet respectively down, together with about a cart load of sharply shivered chips of the pillar. These were scattered over the old surface level, averaging about twelve feet below the present.

Unfortunately none of the portions found bore any inscription, and the onset of the rains put a stop to further search for the season. Renewed search in the following year (January 1897), beyond recovering several more uninscribed fragments, including one at D, added nothing new. Nor was the base of the pillar found as evidence of the exact original site.

The missing inscribed portions of this pillar, I am still hopeful, may be found by further thorough examination of this plot and its neighbourhood—if not the whole inscribed part, at least a portion of it, also let us hope the base of the pillar so as to fix the original position exactly. For the symmetrical position of the site where the broken pieces of the pillar were found, namely, between the two old ponds and adjoining the mass of mediæval brick buildings on the south side of southerly pond, where too lies the coping stone of a Buddhist railing, and the rows of brick cells on either side fringing both ponds, even although these cells seem to have been built in mediæval times after the destruction of the pillar—all these considerations seem to favour the view that hereabouts was the original site of the pillar, and that this was one of the two *Asoka*-pillars seen and described by the Chinese pilgrims.

Which of these two pillars may this one be? The first and most southerly pillar stood at the side of the great relic-*stūpa* (see plan I) by the side of the stone bearing Buddha's foot-prints, and over half-a-mile south of 'the city.' It was 'about 30 feet high'[1] and of great circumference,[2] and it bore at HIUEN TSIANG's visit a "mutilated inscription."

The other and more northerly pillar was 'to the north side of the palace,'[3] 300 or 400 paces north of the first pillar, says FA HIAN, and it was 'several tens of feet high'[4] or 'more than thirty feet'[5] 'with a lion on the top of it. On this pillar there is an inscription recording the things which led to the building of *Ni-li*, with the number of the year, the day, and the month.' But by HIUEN TSIANG's day the hell-legend[6] had been grafted on to this site, and this pillar was shown to this pilgrim as marking the site of the place of torture which ASOKA is alleged in the later myths to have built before his conversion to Buddhism.

Although in the absence of the inscription the identity of this pillar cannot be stated with certainty, there seems a probability, when we work back from *Pānch Pahūri* as our fixed point, that it is the northernmost of the two, or the '*Nili*' or 'hell'-pillar.

Still there remains the possibility that it may be the pillar at the foot-print stone, and in favour of this view is the fact that I found that a great stone lying in the *Bulandhi* grove, about 150 yards to the north-east, had attached to it exactly the same legend as was related to HIUEN TSIANG in regard to the mutilated stone with Buddha's foot-prints : indeed, this was related to me in that pilgrim's very words. Moreover, about 50 yards to the south is the coping stone of a Buddhist railing of perhaps the most primitive type yet found ; and the cross bars of the railing (plate I)

[1] *Records*—ii, 91, and *Life of H. Tsiang*—BEAL, 102. FA HIAN says 'about 3 *chang* high,' which BEAL translates as 35 feet, and LEGGE as 'more than 30 cubits high,' p. 80.

[2] The circumference according to FA HIAN was one and-a-half *chang*, which BEAL translates as '18 feet.'

[3] *Records*—ii, 85 and *Life of H. Tsiang*, BEAL. 102.

[4] *Records*—ii, 85, about 3 *chang*—FA HIAN.

[5] *Fa Hian*—LEGGE, p. 80.

[6] *Id.* 80.

were unearthed in digging a well about 100 yards to the east of the fragments of the pillar, and several others are worshipped in the small temples in the immediate vicinity. But if this be the southerly pillar near the foot-print stone and the great relic-*stūpa*, where are the remains of the latter? The only mound here which suggests a possible *stūpa* is that on which the mosque stands to the north-east of the *Kalu* pond. This might account for the disappearance of many bricks and stones, also the fact that the present grand trunk road, which was also the road for the Pathan soldiery in the Muhammadan period, passes directly through this site, and also the highly embanked railway line, any one or all of which may have used the large brick ruins near as a quarry for road-metal.

*How was this pillar destroyed?* The shaft has been shivered into hundreds of pieces; but the chief line of fracture in the larger pieces shows a vertical cleavage, dividing the pillars almost into two equal halves. This naturally suggests lightning as the destroying agent, and it is remarkable that the *Asoka*-pillar which was discovered in 1896 at Buddha's birth-place, as a result of the representations and indications made by me to Government, shows exactly the same feature, namely, a vertical split down the centre of the column, dividing it into two lateral halves, and in this case the injury certainly was done by lightning, and it had occurred previous to the visit of HIUEN TSIANG, who described it as having been done by 'a wicked [thunder-] dragon.'[1]

We know, however, from the pilgrim that the fanatical Brahmanist king of Western Bengal, ŚAŚĀṄKA, had about twenty years before, overran *Pāṭaliputra* and *Gaya* and destroyed as far as he could the Buddhist monuments. He cut down the sacred *Bodhi* tree at *Buddha-Gaya*, and he especially defaced and destroyed the foot-print stone at *Pāṭaliputra*, but it was 'miraculously' restored. HIUEN TSIANG makes no mention of the destruction of the pillar beside the foot-print stone, and his reference to both

[1] BEAL's tr. II. 25.

pillars as being 'several tens of feet long' and 'thirty feet long' leads to the supposition that they were still erect and unbroken.

The time at which the destruction of this pillar happened seems from the depth of the level of the splinters, namely, about twelve feet, to have been probably before the Muhammadan period.

The row of cells along the north border of the plot containing the fragments of the pillar were found to have one of the fragments under their foundation, thus fixing their relative ages. The plan of these cells is shown in the accompanying sketch.

At the north-east corner of *Kumrāhar* at the point marked 14 on plan II is reported to be a huge trough, about ten feet long and three or four broad, about 15 feet under the surface. FA HIAN states that to the north of ASOKA's palace and not far from the '*Nili*' pillar was "a great stone trough" for the palace-offerings of food to the monks. The site of a colossal buried trough was reported to me by the villagers. Without any leading questions on such a subject, the owner of the field pointed out the spot to me, and his story was corroborated by an old villager. They state that when the present railway (East India main line) was being made about forty years ago, a deep cutting was begun at this point for the subway tunnel. In the digging they came to the white sand of the old river *Sōn*, and at about fifteen feet they reached a great trough of the approximate size above stated, but they say it was of iron, and not stone. It was so heavy that it could not be pulled out despite the superintendence of the European engineer. Ultimately, and especially as the superstitious coolies were alarmed at this monster immovable trough, the cutting was filled up and the present subway was cut, about fifty yards further west.

In view of this circumstantial story I sank a trench at the spot indicated, in March, and soon exposed the old line of cutting through the *Sōn* sand, thus confirming to this extent the report; but as it was so early in the dry season water appeared at nine feet, and the search could not be continued. By May the subsoil

To face page 34

PLATE III

ARCHAIC STONE-RAILING, (WITHOUT COPING BAR.)

Photo by L. A. Waddell.

a. *Side view showing mortise notch.*

Photogravure, Survey of India Offices Calcutta, April 1903.

waters should have sunk sufficiently low to allow of this important trace being searched for. It is quite possible that ASOKA's trough might be of iron: on the other hand, this buried trough may prove to be stone after all.

To the north of this alleged site of the trough and of *Kumrāhar* village, as far as the broad old channel of the *Sōn* in a line with the part called *Gun Sāgar* is a more or less compact mass of old foundations intersected by a few relatively narrow waterways, the most southerly of which we have seen to be palisaded.

The eastern border fringing the *Sivai* lake has three Hindu temples, each containing portions of Buddhist images or Buddhist railings, and an interesting sandstone relief of the Sun-God in *quasi*-Greek style.

Portions of two separate old Buddhist railings of sandstone have been found by me in this locality; and they are of especial interest, not only on account of their extremely primitive character—probably the earliest yet found—but also from their having doubtless surrounded the two chief shrines of *Pāṭaliputra*, namely, the *stūpa* of Buddha's relics and the foot-print of Buddha. Of these two railings thus found, one, apparently the oldest (see plate III) as it has ruder designs and is most weathered, was found in isolated portions, chiefly in the *Dargah*, though two posts were on a mound at *Bahadurpur*. The oldest inhabitant could give no clue as to the point where they were unearthed, though the crossbars are believed to have been dug up at the *Dargah*.

The posts of this railing are of two kinds—one bears central bosses or medallions containing animals, namely, a lion, with a smaller animal, possibly its cub, and a dog or lion-faced sea-monster. The other kind of post bears carved human figures: on one post an amorous couple under a tree, and on another post are depicted evidently the same couple as prisoners tied by a cord.

A chief peculiarity of this railing in addition to its generally primitive appearance is that its cross-bars are rectangular and not ovoid, and they are let into very small mortised sockets, as in ordinary woodwork (see plate V).

The other railing (plate I), of which only two posts, a portion of the coping stone and several bars have yet been found, is in fairly good preservation. The bars were dug out at a point about sixty yards west of the alleged site of the trough in question, while the two posts have been in the house of the landlord of *Kumrāhar* since his father's time, and their source is forgotten. They are of a fine-grained whitish sandstone. Each of the posts is adorned with 3 rosettes, the upper and lower representing varied forms of the lotus flower, and the central one bears an image or a group-picture. The central medallion on one of the upright posts represents a man going uphill with one of the mythical celestial horse-headed females (*Kinnara*), who is carrying a child. What seems to be a fragment of another post is in the neighbouring temple, and bears the figure of a female seated holding an object like a long bag in her lap. The medallion on the square cross-bar seems to represent a scene from the *Jātakas:* a Buddha or sage under a seven-headed snake canopy is standing under a tree with his right hand uplifted, and behind him seems a tripod. At his side are two spouted jars, and a bird sits on a bell-shaped structure, scored as if to represent rocks. The fragment of coping stone represents in its upper moulding a row of bells and beads such as doubtless were tied from post to post of its wooden prototype[1] and in its frieze is sculptured a very crude tree followed by a group of three monks or Buddhas separated by some object from two birds. Altogether the style of sculpture in the railings is very primitive, and seems purely Indian in its details except the bead ornament of the coping stone.

Both rails are sculptured on one side only, the reverse side being plain and rough.. The railing last described has been inserted directly in the ground or in a plastered plinth without

[1] As Dr. BLOCH points out that a similar but more elaborate arrangement is found on the coping of the Bharhut rails.

any stone basement. Both rails are of small size, the posts measuring only 46 and 37 inches in length respectively; and in the more richly ornamented one (plate I) with the ovoid bars, the discs on the pillar are 8″ in diameter. whilst those of the bars is 10″. The fragment of a large post or pillar (fig. 2, plate II) may possibly be the top of a corner post of the railing. It bears on one side under the frame-work of a balcony the uplifted hand evidently of a female grasping a tree, and on the other side the head of a prince surmounted by an umbrella.[1]

The original site of at least one of these railings almost certainly must have been as a fence to the stone containing Buddha's foot-prints. This stone was enshrined by ASOKA in a temple (*vihāra*); if the railings were outside the temple, it would be of considerable size. The other monument most likely to have a railing would be the great relic-*stūpa*. This would be the largest. Unfortunately no part of the railing contains an inscription, not even mason's marks, except the corner post, the top of which bears a few roughly cut weathered characters, of a later age, mostly resembling mediæval *Devanagari*, also 'shell' letters; and there seem to be vestiges of an inscription along the front moulding, but now quite illegible.

*Sandalpur* (4 on plan II) on the northern border of this area of old foundations has portions of old brick walls showing up in the village and adjoining fields when wells are dug, and curiously there is a local tradition that the giant BHIM SEN is associated with the place—nowadays ASOKA's gigantic pillars are usually ascribed by the Hindus to this Brahmanical personage. On the mound close to the east of this village (5 on plan II) and west of the mound of brick-maker's refuse are two small square temple-pillars in polished sandstone. Like the *Asoka*-pillars, both are rectangular. One is about five feet long, and the other is of a stepped pyramidal form, $2\frac{1}{2}$ feet long, each

[1] It seems just possible that this might be 'the crowning jewel' of the relic-*stupa* referred to by HIUEN TSIANG as being of "stone with a surrounding balustrade," see p. 72.

step about a foot deep.[1] They are said to have been found in digging bricks out of this mound, but a trench cut here revealed no bricks *in situ*. To the east of this, a few yards distant, a trustworthy report[2] states that there formerly lay here till about 30 years ago a large stone pillar about eight feet long, bearing an in scription which was popularly said to be 'Chinese,' and around it a large religious fair used to be held annually. This pillar was removed by the owner, and the fair afterwards was given up. Although the owner denied to me all knowledge of the matter, the fact is well attested, and this pillar may probably yet be found in the city. It may have been the missing inscribed fragment of the *Asoka*-pillar.

*Bulandhi* grove to the south of *Sandalpur* is a promising site, and seems to contain some of those palaces with marvellously ornamented walls of stone, the large stones to which FA HIAN refers.[3] My attention was directed to this site by some villagers who asked me to come and see a curious big flat stone that had always existed there, and no matter where it was taken to "it always came back to its old place." Here they used the identical expressions employed by HIUEN TSIANG in regard to the stone with Buddha's foot-prints.

This celebrated stone bearing the foot-prints of Buddha had the following legendary history. When the aged Buddha in his eightieth year, and a few weeks before his death, was leaving for the last time this part of the country, *Magadha*, which had been the scene of his attaining the Buddhahood and of his most notable missionary labours, and which contained his favourite hermitages, and he with truly human nature was obviously wending his way homewards (towards *Kapilavastu*) to die, before entering the boat which was to ferry him over to the north bank of the Ganges, he stood on this stepping-stone at

[1] These stepped pyramids are figured in the early Ananta cave sculpture in Orissa, see also ANDERSON's *Archæology Catalogue, Indian Museum*, I, 78.

[2] Related by Surveyor Ahmad Hossain, who as a child used to play around this stone.

[3] Page 263.

*Pātaliputra*, which at that time as we have seen was only a small village,[1] and exclaimed to his faithful attendant and cousin: "ANANDA! this is the very last time that I shall gaze upon the [land of the] *Vajrāsana* (*i.e.*, *Buddha-Gaya*) and *Rajagriha*," and adds the chronicle "the traces of his feet on this stone remained"[2]

This stone was afterwards enshrined in a temple built by ASOKA who paidit frequent visits, as it was "within his royal precincts;" but shortly before the visit of HIUEN TSIANG'S, that chronicler relates that the stone was broken and defaced by the iconoclast Brahmanical *Raja* SASANKA,[3] who threw it into the Ganges, "but it came back to its old place." It was "a great square stone," and the impression was of the right and left foot, each "about 1 foot 8 inches long and 6 inches broad,"[4] for it was customary to represent Buddha physically as of heroic size; and JULIEN'S translation of the pilgrim's narrative states regarding SASAṄKA'S mutilation:—

> "Se rendit aussitôt dans le lieu ou etait la pierre, et voulut effacer les traces sacrees; mais a peine avait-elle ete taillee *à coups de ciseau* qu'elle redevenait unie, et que les ornaments reparaissaient comme auparavant."[5]

The stone in the *Bulandhi* grove with this curious tradition attached to it, that "it came back to its old place," is a rough block of chipped quartzite about two and-a-half feet square by two feet deep and just such a stone as might be a stepping-stone at a ferry. It bears on its upper surface two slight depressions side by side of what might be considered monster foot-prints, each about twenty inches long by about six inches wide; and it bears marks of hacking or chiselling on its upper surface and sides, though it is much worn, as the villagers for

[1] See his 'prophecy' on page 1.

[2] *Life*, BEAL'S transl. 102.

[3] SASANKA, King of Karna-suvarna in Western Bengal, actively persecuted the Buddhists. He invaded Magadha and murdered by stratagem the King of Kanauj—Rajyavardhana. Inscribed evidence of his invasion is found in a rock-cut seal matrix at *Rhotas* fort on the *Son*. CUNNINGHAM'S *A.S.R.*—and FLEET'S *Corpus Inscrip.* III.

[4] *Idem* 102.

[5] *Voyage*, &c., I, 422.

centuries have been using it as a hone to sharpen their reaping hooks and knives. Still even now I can well imagine a devoted monk like HIUEN TSIANG still able to see, with the eyes of faith, in the dim 'morning light' (for it was only then he saw the details), "figures of flowers and fishes clustering around the toes." This rough block resembles all the really ancient rock-marked 'foot-prints' of Buddha such as at *Mount Uren*, all of which possess a rude naturalness, whereas the neatly chiselled 'prints' on basalt or marble blocks at *Buddha-Gaya* and elsewhere are flagrantly artificial and mostly modern.

In view of the presence of this remarkable stone in the *Bulandhi* grove, although there was no other indication of a building on the level surface, beyond the fine *debris* of bricks, I asked Mr. MILLS to sink a trench by the side of this stone (1 plan II). This disclosed at a depth of twelve feet below the surface the beautiful colossal capital figured (plate III, p. 16). It measures 49 inches long by 33½ inches deep, and it lay at the side of a large thick ancient wall with a stretch of a plastered brick pavement, and curiously amongst some old copper and bronze coins found here was one of the Chinese pattern with a hole in its centre, but its surface so corroded as to be illegible. It was probably dropped or purposely deposited here by a later Chinese Buddhist pilgrim.

This beautifully sculptured capital is of extreme interest, in that while it has a suggestively Ionic outline, it seems to exhibit a transition stage from the early Assyrian of Persepolis to the Corinthian order. It is adorned in Greek style with the typical beading and honeysuckle; and yet it is found at the very head-quarters of ASOKA himself and by its artistic workmanship and the depth at which it was found is probably of ASOKA's own age. In any case it is a telling testimony to the strong Western influence in very early times at *Pāṭaliputra*.

The ancient walls and platforms have only been very partially exposed owing to the depth and consequent expense, but this site is a very promising one.

The villages of *Rampur* and *Bahadurpur* (9 and 10 on map), which rise further west, as islets from the marshy fields bordering the old *Sōn*, are built over mounds of brick *débris*, and in several places lie large blocks of rough unhewn stone about two feet in diameter, not, however, of sufficient size to suggest the massive blocks of Mahendra's hermitage. At *Rampur* Mr. MILLS exposed at the south-west corner of the village about twelve feet below the present surface a series of wooden planks built up one over the other like the trestles of a bridge. This structure is evidently the foundation of a tower or of a jetty or pier projecting into the old *Sōn* river. It was exposed, running north and south, and at its side was a wooden lined drain traced for about sixty yards, the upright beams of which, about eight feet long, are set on a brick-plinth 17 feet below the surface, and the bottom of this waterway was also lined with wood.[1] At *Bahadurpur* I found two of the posts of the old stone-railing already described, lying on the mound at the village temple, and a third at *Rampur*. At the eastern border of *Bahadurpur* an excavation showed deeply buried wooden drains of the same kind as at *Rampur* above noted, but the bed of the channel was paved with brick about 11 inches square. The wood in these cases was *sal*, as with the beam-palisade.

Still further west, about three-quarters of a mile, at *Pirthipur* (11 on map), where chips of granite and other stones were to be seen near the lips of the irrigation-wells, the villagers reported that a large pillar lay buried about ten feet down at the north-eastern corner of the village. On excavation[2] it proved to be part of a massive sandstone pillar evidently belonging to a temple (plate VI, fig. 3). It measured

[1] The detailed plans of this drain as recorded by Mr. MILLS are filed in the Secretariat Office of the Public Works Department for reference.

[2] By Babu Purnachandra Mukerji.

about 5 feet long and 3 feet 6 inches in breadth, and seems to be the base of a pillar. It has a vase-shaped torus surmounting its square stem, from which it is separated by 2 stepped plinths and a constricting band of rope ornament, while the upper margin of the vase is decorated with the conventional Greek petals, and the Ionic beaded moulding of the same kind as on the coping stone of the railing. One face of the square stem bears two lines of indistinct circular characters, somewhat like Burmese. About twenty yards to the north-east, where a mound of bricks cropped up in the fields, excavation revealed a plastered brick-terrace only two and-a-half feet below the surface, and on this were found standing *in situ* the bases of five broken sandstone-posts of a railing. The lines of these posts running north and south and east and west showed that they marked the south-west corner of an angular enclosure. The pillars measured only 8½ inches in breadth and 6½ inches in thickness, so that their original length must have been about three feet. Their cross-bars were oval in shape, $7'' + 3''$, and both the bars and posts were altogether plain and uncarved. About 300 feet to the south-west of this spot were found several large fragments of the top of that squat temple-pillar already described; and 25 feet to the north were exposed at three feet below the surface the outline of some houses evidently mediæval from the size of their bricks. The roughness of the short, square stem and the squatness of the pillar with its bowl-shaped upper extremity almost suggest the possibility that the lower part was sunk in masonry.

The extensive high mound of brick ruins now covered by the Muhammadan settlement of the *Dargah* (9 on map) may be considered with the palace. It is undoubtedly an important Buddhist site, as several portions of old and mediæval Buddhist sculptures have been unearthed when digging foundations here. Some of those plastered into the wall the

*Maulvi* allowed me to remove for Government.[1] Several others are used as lintels and blocks for strengthening walls in various buildings and so are buried out of sight. A large one deeply carved had been utilized by the masons in this way about a week before my visit, and could not be recovered. An elegant column, apparently of the GUPTA period, was dug out at the north-west corner of the mound. It bears an inscription in the mystic and as yet undeciphered so-called 'shell-characters,' of which I took rubbings; the carved post (plate IV, fig. 3) found here also bears an inscription apparently in this character. A remarkable and possibly important structure at the *Dargah* is a stone passage 25 feet down the large ancient well on the borders of the *Gun Sagar*. According to the current tradition it leads to *Bhikna Pahari* on the one side and to the subterranean passage at *Kumrahar* on the other, each of the points being nearly a mile distant. I saw that its orifice on the north-west border of the well had a regularly built lintelled doorway of stone. It was partially covered by water at my visit in March, but in May it is said to be dry. At such a season it was explored for a few yards with a torch several years ago.

The eastern border of the old palace appears to have been probably in the line running the western border of the *Sivai* lake (14 on map) through *Dhanuki*, on the eastern margin of *Kumrāhar*, to *Chhoti Pahari* (26 on map) with eastern fortified offshoot to the *Maharaj khunda* or 'Emperor's moats' (19 on map) at *Tulsi Mandi*, where were found the cluster of beam-palisades and large stones marking apparently the position of a tower as already described. Near the south of this latter point (20 on map and 19 on plan II) is the celebrated holy well, called the '*Agam Kuan*.'

[1] Thus were obtained the carved post (plate II, fig. 3) and door jamb, the cross-bars of railing (plate V), a scroll architrave, evidently of ASOKA's age. Of those still fixed in walls is the image of the preaching Buddha which is in old sandstone and is extremely interesting in that the attitude of the fingers is identical with that still figured conventionally by the Japanese and Tibetans in representing certain mystical Buddhas.

This sacred well, the name of which literally seems to mean 'the Fiery Well,' appears to me to be a surviving vestige of the so-called 'hell' of ASOKA with its fiery cauldrons, which the later monkish legend credited ASOKA with having deliberately made to torture poor people, Nero-like, in the days before his conversion to Buddhism.[1] What we know, however, of ASOKA as a brave soldier and kind-hearted man goes quite against the credibility of this story, and the reference in his edict-inscription (No. VIII) that 'in past days the Kings went on pleasure excursions, stag-hunting, &c.,' the simple tone of such passages, as Dr. KERN well says, is "calculated to awaken in us the conviction that the atrocities attributed by the later Buddhists to their benefactor rests upon a misunderstanding. The stories of both the Northern and Southern Buddhists to which it is usual to give the specious name of 'traditions' differ among themselves to such an extent as to be suspicious on that ground alone. The ninety-nine-fold fratricide committed, as is stated by ASOKA, is related with such circumstantiality that its untruth is palpable. The story of the Northern Buddhists is different, but if possible still more inept. According to them, Asoka at the beginning of his reign caused a place of torture to be built in order to torment poor creatures and so forth. Now the King himself stated in the first tablet that at the beginning of his reign[2] he permitted the death of innocent creatures, *i.e.*, their slaughter for food. Is it not in the highest degree probable that the hell for the torture of poor animals is a misrepresentation, intentional or otherwise, of the slaughter-house? The contrast between the hell built by the prince before his conversion and the monasteries built by him after that event was too striking for so splendid an opportunity for a display of bigotry to be allowed to pass. In the midst of the conflicting variations which have sprung up under the clumsy hands of the monks without humour or imagination, without feeling or a love of truth, we can yet distinguish a

[1] See Appendices IV and V. Also BURNOUF'S *Introd. Ind. Buddhisme.*

[2] The edict says 'kings,' which may be taken to include ASOKA and his practices before his conversion.

uniform theme which may be thus expressed. In his youth Asoka gave himself up to depraved passions, to *vyasanáni* (to which the chase belongs), he had shown no mercy to innocent creatures (*i.e.*, deer, &c.) was 'cruel,' a *Chanda* ASOKA. But after his conversion he bade farewell to his sinful life, gave himself up exclusively to 'righteousness' and became a *Dharma*-ASOKA."[1]

This material 'hell,' however, was one of the sights of the ruined palace at the time of HIUEN TSIANG's visit,[2] and it was described as having contained fiery cauldrons and fearsome ovens for terrible torture.

Curiously the very same legend, which the Chinese pilgrim records in regard to its torture-chamber, is still related by the *Jain* priests of the temple adjoining this *Agam* well. They tell, how a monk named SUDARSAN was thrown by the king of *Paṭaliputra* into a fiery furnace in the neighbourhood (the exact spot of which, however, they have forgotten); but he remained unscathed and was found seated serenely on a throne of lotuses, to the astonishment of the king who ordered his release and afterwards patronised him and established him in the immediate neighbourhood.[3]

The current popular legend of this *Agam* well or pit associates the place both with heat and with hell. It is regarded with horror, and though actively venerated, its water is never drunk. It is especially worshipped during the hot weather, beginning with the onset of the hot winds in March and lasting for four months. During these months, and especially on the 8th day of each month, troops of women and children come bringing offerings of money and flowers which they throw into the well, and they especially pray for protection against the disfiguring

[1] *Indian Antiquary*, V. 265.

[2] *See* page 72 para 11, also Appendix IV page 76.

[3] This legend of ASOKA's hell possibly also owes its origin in part to a false etymology of the name of the city *Pāṭaliputra*, as this word leads itself so readily to the idea of hell. '*Patala*' is the ordinary Hindu hell and *putra* (properly *puttra*) is the Vedic word for a 'Son' in the literal sense of a 'deliverer (of his father) from hell,' as according to the well-known Brahmanical belief it is a religious obligation for a man to beget a son, as only a son can deliver (*tra*) a man's spirit from the hell of purgatory (*put*) into which it falls immediately after death, hence the religious title of a son is *put* + *tra*.

fever of small-pox. The largest gathering is on the *Agri mela* on the eighth day of the month of *Asarh* (May-June) at which over 100,000 people attend and goats are sacrificed. The modern legend also associates it with the Indian hell, alleging that the well leads down to hell in the centre of the earth, and that a heavy piece of wood which was lost in the ocean was found by a sage down this well, which, according to the local Brahmanical etymology, means 'the bottomless' pit (*Agaham*), though the word is never so pronounced by the people themselves.

The great antiquity of this pit or 'well' is undoubted. It is reported to have been a custom in the early Muhammadan rule, since 700 years ago, for every newly-arrived Muhammadan official to proceed to the well and throw in a gold or silver coin according to the wealth of the individual.

It seems to me to be a vestige of Asoka's "hell;" and its position here, between the palace and the old city and adjoining *Tulsi 'Mandi,'* which name implies the market-place of the king, is in keeping with the possibility that here was the site of the royal slaughter-house or out-kitchen which, as Dr. Kern suggests, was in after days transformed by the life-cherishing Buddhist monks into a hell where ASOKA wantonly condemned innocent lives to a horrible death.

Due south of this pit or well, about half-a-mile, is a very old site called *Kharaunia* (21 on plan II) now uninhabited. It is in series with a strip of high land connecting more or less continuously the *Chhoti Pahārī* mound with *Patna.* At its north-western corner (20 on plan II) is the cluster of old beams already noted as being about 18 feet below the surface and probably forming the foundation of one of the old wooden towers of the fortifications. The brick-remains seem confined to the lower half of this mound; but the walls which I traced were evidently mediæval, only, judging from their being only about three feet from the surface and built of medium-sized bricks.

A very striking high line brick building running east and west (22 on plan II) connects this mound with the much larger mound of *Chhoti Pahāri*. It appears to me to be an old viaduct or a *via sacra*, leading from the city across an old channel of the *Sōn* to the sacred monuments and the monasteries in their immediate neighbourhood. For, what must have been one of the principal of these monuments, namely, the great *stupa* (24 on plan II) is only about 200 yards from the western end of this high brick embankment and it must have been visited by thousands of people every day from *Pāṭaliputra* bringing offerings of flowers as at the very similarly sized *stūpa* at Rangoon, the *Shwe-Dagon*.

The importance of this great *stūpa*, owing to its being practically the only old building of ASOKA's period at Patna of which any large portion is yet found to exist, nowadays, and its position amidst the ruins of so many large brick buildings and with reference to the position of the *Pānch-Pahāri* mound on the south and the fragments of the pillar of ASOKA to its north-west, all suggesting the probability that it might be, as General Cunningham had conjectured, the first and greatest of all the *stūpas* which ASOKA built to enshrine Buddha's relics, rendered the examination of this mound especially desirable.

That *stūpa* was a ruin even in HIUEN TSIANG's day. He thus describes it:—"Its foundation-walls are sunk[1] and it is in a leaning, ruinous condition. There remains, however, the crowning jewel of the cupola. This is made of carved stone, and has a surrounding balustrade. This was the first of the 84,000 (*stūpas*) and ASOKA *Rāja* erected it by the power of man in the middle of his royal precinct. It contains a *ching*[2] of relics of the *Tathāgatha* (Buddha)."[3] And FA HIAN noted that it was 300—400 paces south of the hell. It is a curious illustration of history repeating itself to find that within the British rule a mammoth structure was reared in ASOKA's old capital which

[1] JULIEN translates this (I, p. 416): Il s'est enfonce en terre, et il neu resté plus que la coupole qu'on a couverte de riches ornaments et entourée d'une balustrade en pierre.

[2] A *ching* = 53 centilitres according to M. Natalis Rondot (in JULIEN *Memoires* I, 418). This would give ·933 pints, or 32·34 cubic inches of Buddha's relics.

[3] See Appendix IV.

repeated the huge dome-like form of the early *stūpas.* Thus that great brick building at *Bankipur*, called the '*Gola*,' which was intended to be used as a corn-store, as in the days of the Pharoahs, to protect the country against famine,[1] recalls the bee-hive form of ASOKA's great *stūpas.*

Inspection of this great mound at *Chhoti Pahāri* (24 in plan II) showed at once that it was undoubtedly part of a great *stūpa.* The villagers in removing its bricks for building purposes, as they have used it as a quarry for centuries, had disclosed this fact by exposing a considerable surface of the solid brickwork, consisting of the characteristic courses of large bricks, 18″×12″×2½″. The bricks are well made and burnt, and mostly of a brilliant scarlet colour. A little scraping away of the surface *débris* was sufficient to show that the mass of brickwork was still about 20 feet above the present ground level and its top measured over 60 feet across, but it was divided by a great lane which had been roughly quarried through it from east to west near its apparent centre. This destructive cutting is said to have been made in 1895. That so much of the *stūpa* still remains is mainly owing to the top being crowned by Muhammadan graves, and also by a small Hindu shrine, where one of the small stone columns from the ruins is worshipped as *Mahadeva.*

In order to trace the outline of this *stūpa* and see whether or not its core was still intact, and to try to recover any inscriptions, which doubtless were originally present, I cleared away the *débris* from the top, and also by means of a few trenches, from its sides. This latter operation, however, was very costly and tedious, owing to the great depth to which these trenches had to be carried—15 to 25 feet—and the scrupulous care taken to destroy no part of the structure, but only to remove the overlying rubbish and broken fragments of ages. This examination showed that the exploration of this *stūpa* was beset by

[1] This *gola* or 'granary' was built in 1786 "for the perpetual prevention of famine," says its inscription, by Captain John Garstin (who died a Major-General in 1820 and lies buried in Park Street Cemetery of Calcutta), but it never was used, and remains 'a useless monument of a mistake.' Its hollow interior possesses a weird echo exaggerating and repeating tremulously the slightest sound.

To face page 48. 

1.

2

3.

VIEW OF THE GREAT STUPA MASONRY.

1. View from quarry in 1895: (a) Site of cross-laid brick column (b) Lingam.
2. Larger view of masonry at cross-laid brick column.
3. Pillar terminal, bearing inscriptions in "shell" characters reduced to ⅙th.

Photo by L.A. Waddell. Photogravure, Survey of India Offices, Calcutta April 1903.

PLAN IV.

# Showing Excavations at the Great Stupa at Chhoti Pahāri.

(To face page 48.)

REFERENCES.

The *dotted lines* indicate the exploratory trenches made in March 1899.

The *red* tinted portions represent structural masonry found *in situ*.

The *figures* give the elevation of the latter above the mean river level at Patna.

The vertically shaded portion is the deep hole quarried out in 1895.

The ✕ marks site of the cross laid brick column (see Plate IV, Figs. *a* & *b*).

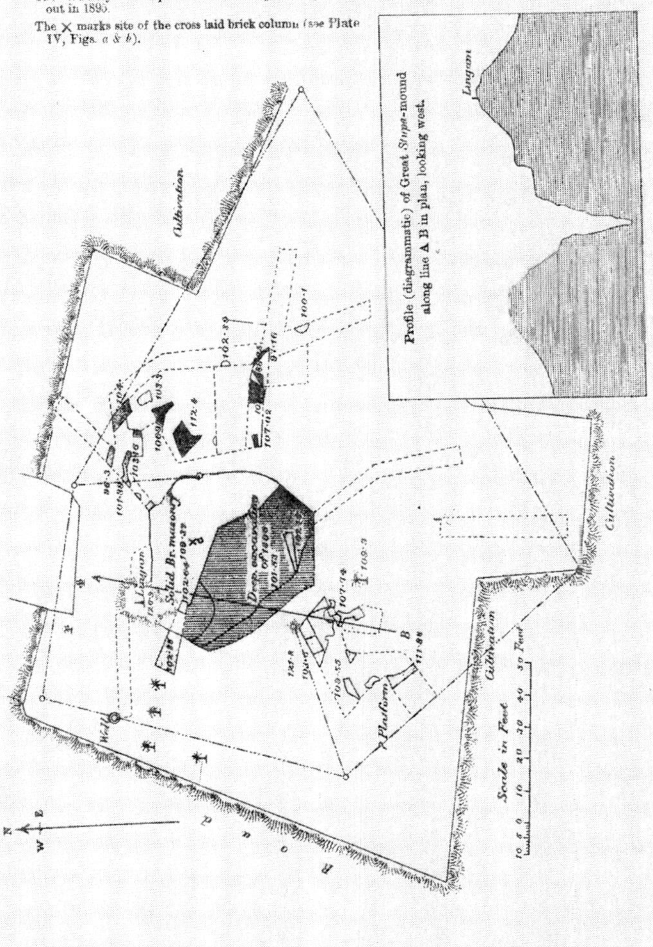


L. A. WADDELL.

the unusual difficulty that there was absolutely none of the usual concentric arrangement of the bricks so as to supply a clue to the centre or to the circumference of the building. The bricks were all laid with thin plaster and mud in straight lines (see plate IV*a* and *b*), and the sides of the *stūpa* were so honeycombed and irregularly riddled by the holes made by the brick-diggers that no decided clue could be readily found to the circumference by the deep trenches on the margin. Several apparent curves which were found are noted on the attached plan, and there also are shown several level portions which might be procession-paths improvised at later ages when the *stūpa* had become a ruin, or they may merely be courses peeled up, by the brick-diggers. To settle these points definitely would require more elaborate and costly excavation.

These preliminary excavations showed that the highest part of the existing brickwork was 23 inches above the present ground level, and at this height was another point 34 feet to its north-west, but the main mass of the remaining fabric was 18 feet above the present ground level. It was also found that the northern end had been quarried away bodily, so that this side of the mound was steeply scarped. From its general contour and in the light of these side trenches it appeared that this *stūpa* must have been of the enormous size of a hundred feet or more in diameter, and it seemed possible that the great lane which had been driven through it had not reached its centre, and that the centre which in all probability contained inscriptions of immense importance for the history of India might yet be intact. To try to determine this point I began clearing out the rubbish from the deep lane; but as my official duties called me back to Calcutta before this could be completed, I made over this research to Mr. C. R. Wilson, the Principal of Patna College, whose excavations of old Fort-William are well known and whose report on the further excavation of this *stūpa* is appended.[1]

[1] Appendix VI.

Mr. Wilson found that the great cutting went down 25 feet until it reached the mud. On clearing the top of the brickwork bordering the north of this cutting and removing a few layers of the bricks to expose a clean surface, he found that one brick was deliberately laid crosswise to the course of the others (see plate IV*b*). It lay due north and south and it was packed in its position with plastered mud and broken brick. This it was hoped might prove a clue to the centre and be the covering of the central pipe which in the older *stūpas* passes down to the relic chamber. After photographing this noteworthy fact in the structure of this remarkable *stūpa*, Mr. Wilson carefully removed this brick and found that another was laid in exactly similar fashion immediately below it and so on for five courses, then all traces disappeared, as below this point the bricks were laid like the rest, namely, in straight rows without any trace of concentric arrangement. Carefully reviewing the meagre and conflicting indications afforded by this clearing away of the rubbish, Mr. Wilson sank a well at the point marked (on plan III) and at great personal inconvenience carefully watched this excavation down to the foundation mud without however finding the centre, or any object of interest.[1]

Although, then, this *stūpa* is probably the original great relic *stūpa*, and therefore possibly contains inscriptions of immense historical importance, its exploration still remains unfinished. Its full exploration carefully conducted so as to preserve at the same time its remaining structure will be very costly, and is of exceptional difficulty owing to its peculiarity of construction, and the immense depth to which it is embedded in its own ruins and in those of the buildings which surrounded it. Probably it could be undertaken as a famine-relief work in the event of famine ever visiting *Patna* city.

The buildings which surrounded this fabric were evidently monasteries. Fa Hian expressly states that "by the side of the

[1] Mr. Wilson had to leave the same day on which the mud was reached, but Ahmad Hossain now informs me that some brickwork still continued beyond this point, so this ought to be examined before the well is filled up.

*tope* (*stūpa*) of ASOKA there has been built a *Mahāyāna* monastery very grand and beautiful; there is also a *Hīnayāna* one, the two together containing six hundred or seven hundred monks." These buildings thus described as surrounding the great relic-*stūpa* are shown in plan I. They included the stepping-stone with Buddha's foot-prints and its temple, and also the great edict pillar recording ASOKA's great gifts to Buddhism and the *stūpa* marking where the previous Buddhas had rested, which doubtless was at the site of the village *chaitya* where we are told Buddha dwelt during his short stay here.[1] This stepping-stone with the foot-print has already been referred to in connection with *Bulandhi Bagh* where a large stone exists with a similar legend to that related by HIUEN TSIANG in regard to the foot-print stone seen by him. The stepping-stone with the foot-prints lay to the west of the old village. The chronicle records: "The Blessed One left the village (*Pāṭali*) by the western gate, then turning northward he passed the Ganges at a ferry and these were called 'Gotama's Gate' and 'Gotama's ferry.'"[2] This stepping-stone, together with the great relic-*stūpa* itself, are reported by that pilgrim to have been "*in the middle of his* (ASOKA's) royal precinct." Strictly speaking, this *stūpa* at *Chhoti Pahāri* would seem to be rather on the borders of the old palace than within the latter, unless the whole of these monuments, even down to 'The five *stūpas*' (*Pānch Pahāri*), were included within the palace fortifications.

The general grouping and broad outlines of the buildings in this area may be seen in plan II. The viaduct from *Pāṭaliputra* (21) leads by the great mound of *Chhoti Pahāri* (23) to the higher mound of this ruined *stūpa* (24), which is surrounded by several terraces of brick ruins, and at its southern border, (25) a small temple with fragments of Buddhist images, and a portion

[1] The aged Buddha at his visit in his 79th year, dwelt '*in*' the *Chaitya*, and the Burmese commentary (BIGANDET *Legend*, 257) states that it was a *dzeat* or travellers' hall, erected by king AJATASATRU for the reception of the embassy of *Licchavi* princes from *Vaisāli*, and that Buddha on entering the hall took his seat against the central pillar. *Cf.* also DAVID's *Sacred Books* of East, XI; BEAL *idem.*, XIX, 249; Tibetan version in *Dulva* (*Vinaya*), XI, 545*a*, and ROCKHILL's Life, 126.

[2] ROCKHILL's *Life*, 128, also DAVID's *Mahaparinvivāṇa Sutta*.

of a carved basalt facing of a *stūpa.* Whilst to the east below the broad terrace of brick ruins stretches out for nearly a quarter of a mile up to the old river bed the traces of a broad stone pavement. This pavement, consisting of huge flags of stone, about 2 to 3 feet long by about 2 feet broad and 2 inches thick, can be traced about three to four feet under the surface, over about a square quarter of a mile. It doubtless was a great court for processions, as well as a pier, probably within the palace grounds.

To the north of this stone pavement is the mound called *Patharia* or 'the Stony.' It consists mainly of broken brick, with a few traces of walls, which are evidently mediæval.

To the south of the buildings immediately surrounding the great *stūpa*, the mass of brick ruins at (26), now mostly covered by the village of *Bara Pahāri*, or 'the great hill,' probably represent the 'little mountain' built by ASOKA for his great high priest, UPAGUPTA, who I find is evidently the same as the 'MOGALLIPUTTA TISSA' of the Ceylonese.[1] It appears that[2] it was UPAGUPTA who advised ASOKA to erect gigantic *stūpas* throughout India, and who personally conducted that Emperor to the sacred Buddhist spots. The circumstances of his visit to ASOKA at *Pāṭaliputra*, which I detail in an appendix,[3] throw an interesting side light on the personality of ASOKA. To accommodate him and his disciples ASOKA is reputed by HIUEN TSIANG to have built to the north-east of the 'Five Relic *Stupas*' an artificial hill "in the crags and surrounding valleys (of which) there are several tens of *stone* dwellings." The ruins here on the surface of the village are all of brick. There are several large stones in some of the houses hereabout.

The mound of 'The five *stūpas*' is undoubtedly represented by the *Pānch Pahāri* (27 on plan II). HIUEN TSIANG's description is "a collection of five *stupas.* The foundations are

[1] See Appendix VII.
[2] In the semi-historical 'Asoka-legend;' see Appendix VIII.
[3] Appendix VIII.

lofty but ruinous; what remains, however, is a good height. At a distance they look like little hills. Each of them is several tens of paces in front. Men in after days tried to build on the top of these little stūpas......(which) ASOKA erected with exceptional grandeur...... Some disciples of little faith talking together argued thus:—"In old time NANDA *Rāja* built these five (*stūpas*) as treasure-places for his wealth. In consequence of this gossip in after time a king of insincere faith and excited by his covetousness came with his followers to dig (the *stūpas*)."

The evidence that this 'collection' of 'five little hills' is represented by the mound of *Pānch Pahāri* is absolutely convincing. Not only is this fact denoted in its name, which means 'the five hills,' but the structure of the mound reveals that of great *stūpas*, and so late as AKBAR's day (1556—1603 A.D.) the component five elements were still apparent. The contemporary Muhammadan history, kindly translated for me by Dr. STEIN,[1] states that before attacking the rebel army in *Patna* "the Emperor (AKBAR) went out upon an elephant to reconnoitre the fort and the environs of the city, and he ascended the *Panj Pahārī*, which is opposite the fort. *This Panj Pahārī is* [a collection of] *five 'domes'* (*gumbaz*) *which the infidels in old times constructed with hard bricks* [placed] *in layers* [or rows]. The Afghans who were on the walls and bastions of the fortress saw the Emperor and his suite as he was making the survey, and in their despair and recklessness they fired some guns at the *Panj Pahārī*, but they did no injury to any one." In describing this interesting event where the great Moghul ascended the ruins of the massive monuments built by his great prototype ASOKA, his historian uses for these monuments the very word which is used by Muhammadans for the great *stūpas* in Northern India and Afghanistan, namely, *gumbaz*. Moreover, a large incision which

[1] As ELLIOT's translation of the text (*Tabaqāt-i Akbarī*) read rather vaguely "with burnt bricks in five stages," Dr. STEIN looked up the passage in the *MS.* in the Asiatic Society's library, and in his translation of the extract, above given, has placed all explanatory words added by him in square brackets.

was made into the southern side of the mound in 1896 showed unmistakeably the remains of solid brickwork of two great *stūpas* side by side—one to the east of the other. But it was a mere shell, having been dug so freely into, and it still is being dug fitfully into, for the hidden treasure of the old *rāja*, just as related in HIUEN TSIANG's day; and as in his day also they still build upon it. Curiously too I found under a tree in the neighbourhood a small basalt image of the prototype of this Indian Midas, the wealthy NANDA,[1] namely, the burly Buddhist god of wealth, *Jambhala*, sitting over his hoards of treasure and holding a mongoose, which, as the master of the treasure-guarding snakes (the *Nāgas*), symbolises wealth. Upon this image was cut the Buddhist creed in mediæval characters.

Whilst these '5 *stūpas*' were the most southerly of the monuments bordering the old palace, the most northerly was the artificial hillock built by ASOKA for his young brother, Prince MAHENDRA, the monk. It is described by HIUEN TSIANG as "a large stone house. It looks outside like a great mountain, and within it is many tens of feet wide. This is the house which ASOKA *Rāja* commanded the genii to build for his brother who had become a recluse . . . . . . . . . a half-brother called Mahendra . . . . . . . . . The King said: 'If you wish to subdue your heart in quiet you have no need to live in the mountain fastness (of the distant *Rājgir* hills). To meet your wishes I shall construct you a dwelling.'" The dimensions of the artificial stony hill which ASOKA thus constructed are described by FA HIAN as "a greatstone mountain . . . . . . (of stones) four or five paces square, and at the base of the mountain with five great square

[1] Although NANDA is usually considered a historical king of Pāṭali putra several generations subsequent to Buddha. Thus in the Brahmanical drama (*Mudrā-Rākshasa*—WILSON's *Hindu Theatre*, II, 169 :—

> "This is the reign of CHANDRAGUPTA, not
> Of NANDA. To his avaricious soul
> Your treasures were acceptable, but now
> Your king esteems your happiness his wealth."

Nevertheless his legend is referred to in the *Jātakas* which purport to have been recited by Buddha with reference to antecedent times. In the *Nanda-Jātaka* (DAVID's Buddhist Birth Stories, 324) "NANDA, the base-born," is associated with buried treasure.

stones to make a rock chamber, in length about 35 feet and in breadth 22 feet and in height 11 feet or so"[1]

In this regard I have already noted how I found that the name of the "Mendicant Prince" is still associated with an image of a hill-like image which stood on the top of the mound called 'The Mendicant Monk's Hill' (1 and 2 on map) to the north-west of the palace ruins at *Kumrāhar*. As the great mound of *Bhikna Pahari*, which is now crowned by the *Nawab's* residence, consists of brick, so far as could be seen from the incision made into an unoccupied corner of it, it does not appear itself to be the hill of ASOKA's brother Prince MAHENDRA, but the association of the name of 'the mendicant prince' with the image here suggests that it is in the neighbourhood. Very curiously a Hindu ascetic, a *Sunyasi*, who was there, said that a current legend asserts that a subterranean passage leads from this mound to the *Barabar* caves in *Gaya*, where, it will be remembered, is a rock-cut inscription of ASOKA's grandson. And we have seen some evidence of a deep subterraneous passage leading in this direction to the *Dargah* and *Kumrāhar* one to two miles distant. In the garden adjoining the image in question are said to lie great stones which have been struck on digging wells. The tops of several huge stones, such as may have formed a part of this rocky mound, are to be seen in a Muhammadan graveyard about 100 yards to the west of this mound.

Prince MAHENDRA, who according to the Chinese accounts was the young half-brother of ASOKA, is reported by the less trustworthy Ceylonese tradition to be the son of that monarch, yet it is curious that even the latter tradition admits that ASOKA had an only surviving young brother named 'TISSO,' who also was a Buddhist monk, having been ordained in the fourth year of Asoka's reign.[2] As Mahendra is represented to have been the apostle of Buddhism to Ceylon, his precociousness

[1] FA HIAN: Beal I, lvii; see Appendix IV.

[2] *Mahavamso* TURNOUR's 34. ASOKA is represented as having killed all his brothers save this one. *M.* 21—23.

is remarked on. He took only three years to learn the whole Buddhist canon, and he learnt it from the lips of a teacher—not from books.[1] Ceylon, however, is not the only Buddhist country which claimed to have got its Buddhism directly from the son of the greatest Buddhist monarch. For Khoten, across the Central Asian deserts, claims the same,[2] and like Ceylon it also asserts that Buddha himself visited its country.[3]

The excavation on the western border of this mound showed that the mass consisted of broken bricks, and at a depth of 17 feet was reached traces of several walls and plastered platforms of a large building, which evidently had occupied the centre of the mound, but as this was fully built over, permission was not accorded to undermine the houses for this search. This 'hill of the mendicant monk' may therefore be one of the 'hundred' ruined monasteries to which HIUEN TSIANG refers. Possibly in this neighbourhood, though more probably nearer the Ganges river, is the relic-*stūpa* enshrining half the body of Buddha's favourite attendant and cousin, ANANDA, which was erected in *Pāṭaliputra*[4] by the King of *Magadha*, AJATASATRU. Possibly the railing at *Pirthipur* may have belonged to this *stūpa*.

The current vulgar legend amongst the semi-aboriginal *Dusadh* caste who especially worship the image entitled 'the Mendicant Prince' is that *Bhikna* was the watchman of the great mound of *Bhikna Pahāri* and gave his name to it, and that he had a brother called *Pānch* or 'The Five,' who gave his name to the *Pānch Pahāri* mound, and that a Brahman named *Kuṅwār* or 'the prince,' who was an intimate friend of *Bhikna*, and that both were killed here and so are worshipped. This is interesting as showing that both the name *Bhikna* ('monk') and *Kuṅwār* ('prince') are recognised as being the names or titles of men.

[1] *Mahav.* 37; *Dipavaṁsa*, VIII, 28—31.
[2] ROCKHILL'S *Life of Buddha*, 203, 230.
[3] ROCKHILL'S *Life*, etc., 232.
[4] Tibetan *Dulva*, XI, 684-7, and ROCKHILL'S *Life*, etc., 167.

PLATE V
(to face p. 56).

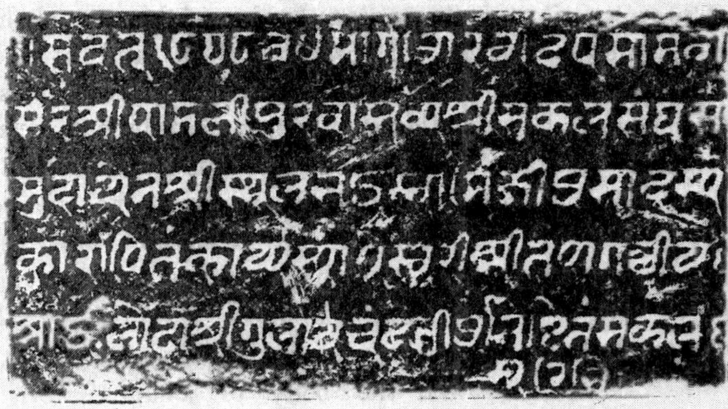

L. A. Waddell.

INSCRIPTION IN JAIN TEMPLE AT PATALIPUR.
From an impression taken by Lieut. Colonel L. A. Waddell.

Reg. No. 783 Bengal, Gl. Dept.—Mar. 08.—800

Photo. S. I. O., Calcutta

The remaining chief monuments and sites outside the palace are the *Kukkuṭarama* monastery, and its surrounding (see plan I), the site of the 'heretics.'

The two oldest monasteries of *Pāṭaliputra* appear to have been 'The Monastery of the Cock' (*Kukkuṭarama*)[1] and the *Asokarama*.[2] The former of these, which lay to the south-east of the city, is also said to have been built by ASOKA[3] and was "a pattern of majestic construction. He gathered there a thousand priests," and here it was that in the closing days of his life, when he seems to have been deposed from power, he, poverty-struck, offered half an *Amlaka* fruit[4] to the priests, which event was afterwards marked by a *stupa*. The location of this building, as I previously indicated in 1892, seems about 33 on the map, where there are several mounds not yet explored.

The 'heretics,' that is, the *Jains*, are mentioned in relation to a spot 'to the north-west' of this *stūpa*. Curiously this brings us exactly to the *Jain* temples at *Kamaldah* (21 on map), where in the highest of the temples I found the following important inscription, containing the name *Paṭalipura* and referring to a well-known *Jain* saint of ancient *Paṭaliputra* who lived in the third century B.C. This inscription (see plate V), which I roughly translated in my report of 1892, has been critically translated for me by Dr. T. Bloch: see appendix, page 83.

This saint is *Sthula-bhadra*, who was, according to JACOBI,[5] the patriarch of the early *Jain* church in the first part of the third

[1] This is to be distinguished from '*The Cock's foot Monastery*,' so called after a hill of that name about 10 miles east of Gaya. The hill in question, where MAHAKASYAPA was transfigured, evidently obtained its curious name as a descriptive appellation. For I found it has when seen from the north a profile like a cock's foot. The head monk of the "Monastery of the Cock" in ASOKA's early days was YAŚAS the *Sthavira* (*Mahāv.*, 30).

[2] The '*Sthavira* INDAGUTTA' assisted in building it, says the Ceylonese *Mahavam* (34), but the name probably here intended was UPAGUPTA.

[3] *Records*; see appendix; also *Life of Hiuen Tsiang*, 103.

[4] "*Aonla*" in Hindustani, the fruit of *Embolica myrobalans*.

[5] *Sacred Books of the East*, XXII, XLIII.

century B.C. at the time when the canon of the *Svetambara* sect was collected by the council or *Sangha* of *Pāṭaliputra*. He had the title of *Ārya* or 'Sublime,' and was of the *Gautama* clan (*gotra*) and the seventh patriarch in succession from MAHAVIRA,[1] and according to the local tradition he died at this spot, which is now a favourite place of pilgrimage amongst the *Jains*. It is built on a high mound of old brick ruins, about 15 feet above the surrounding level.

In the lower temple is a shrine dedicated to *Seth* SUDARSAN *Swami-ji*, where the attendant priest paints every morning a fresh foot-print in saffron on a block of stone, and near the door is a *pinda* or food offering to the fierce deity, *Bhairab*

The local legend of these two saints was thus given to me by the attendant priest:

STHULA-BHADRA was a celebrated devotee of the *Jaina* order. He was for twelve years exposed here to the fascinating temptation of one *Kosiya*,[2] and successfully passing this ordeal he died here, and this temple was erected to his memory. The story of the other saint I find repeats the leading feature, the legend of ASOKA's miraculous conversion. SUDARSAN is said to have been a *Jain* devotee, who preceded STHULA-BHADRA, and through the intrigues of the wife of the king of *Pāṭaliputra*, was condemned by the king to be burned at the stake; but he was miraculously preserved unharmed by the fire, and appeared in the midst of the flames coolly seated on a throne of lotuses. The terror-struck king besought his pardon and endowed him with a plot of ground here beside the pool, which is hence called *Kamal-dah*, or 'the Lotus-lake,' and here the saint died, and his retreat and tomb became favourite places of Jain pilgrimage

A reference to this spot is said to be contained in the vernacular Jain guide to places of pilgrimages, but I was not able to procure a sight of a copy of this work.

The coins found in these excavations were copper and silver, of no later date than the *Indo-Scythian* of the first and second centuries of our era. A few coins of the *Gupta* period were also obtained. Here, if anywhere, are likely to be found coins

[1] *Id.*, 287.

[2] A *biswa* or courtesan.

of Asoka, if any such ever existed, though hitherto there is no trace of this monarch having indulged in these cherished symbols of sovereignty. Gold coins are not unfrequently found by the villagers, but the latter melt them up immediately through fear of the penalties attaching to the procedure under the Treasure Trove Act. I reported to the police more than one such recent find, but the coins were never recovered; and such valuable clues are yearly disappearing.

## Summary of Results.

The results of this research are already important historically, and to some extent also geographically. One of the most promising of all the lost sites for the recovery of the early history of India has been found together with some of its monuments. Where no trace of the sculptured stones of Asoka's great capital was suspected to exist a few years ago, there have now been unearthed many of the actual sculptures, some of which seem to be quite the oldest yet found in India, and others amongst the oldest; there has been found a colossal pillar of Asoka, of about 250 B.C., lying deeply buried and unsuspected, close to the main line of the East Indian Railway with its rushing trains of nineteenth century passengers. In respect to the question of the indebtedness of the early civilization of Ancient India to the West, there has been unearthed amongst other objects a colossal capital of *quasi*-Ionic style, with Assyrian conventional ornamentation. This, the most Greek thing perhaps yet found in India, except the friezes in Asoka's edict-pillars and the later so-called 'Græco-Buddhist' sculptures of the Panjab, has been found in Asoka's own capital, in the heart of India, and is probably of Asoka's own epoch. The old city and palace boundaries have been defined in several places by means of what seems to be the vestiges of the ancient beam-palisade as described by Megasthenes and by other topographical and excavated features; and several of the important sites located have been beyond all doubt.

With the information thus now made available, it is possible to take up the excavation of the more promising sites in detail, so as to recover inscriptions. For this, however, as with SCHLIEMANN'S excavations at Troy, it will be necessary to dig very deeply, as the structures lie hidden deep down in the accumulated mud and *débris* of over twenty-two centuries.

The hurried circumstances under which this report was written, namely, in the brief intervals snatched from my engrossing official duties, may, I trust, excuse its short comings

In conclusion, I may perhaps be permitted, to express the obligations under which students of Indian History are placed to Sir John Woodburn, K.C.S.I., Lieutenant-Governor of Bengal, and his Secretary, the Hon'ble F. A. Slacke, for the interest they have shown in this exploration, and their generous grant of funds; to the Hon'ble C. E. Buckland, C.I.E., for his cordial assistance when Secretary to Government; also to Mr. Bourdillon, C.S.I., who as Commissioner of Patna afforded several facilities for this research. My acknowledgments are due to Mr. Chalmers, Superintendent of Government Printing, Bengal, for the trouble he has taken in the printing and in improvising several accented types for the transliteration of vernacular names.

CHINA EXPEDITIONARY FORCE;<br>
HONG-KONG,<br>
*26th July 1900.*

# APPENDICES.

## I.

## THE MAURYA DYNASTY.

IN a description of the great capital of the powerful *Maurya* dynasty it would be desirable to give a sketch of the dynasty itself. Unfortunately very little else is yet known about it, besides what has been mentioned in the foregoing text.

The origin and designation of this dynasty, founded at *Pāṭaliputra* by CHANDRA-GUPTA, the grandfather of ASOKA, are involved in deep obscurity. The traditional Buddhistic accounts state that the name is derived from the home of CHANDRA-GUPTA's father, which was called *Mayūra-nagara* or *Moriya-nara*[1] and means 'the Town of Peacocks,' and that it was situated 'on the borders of the Himalaya Mountains;' that its exact site is not specified, though we have seen that it probably was in the extreme north of India and in contact with Assyrian or Greek civilization. The Brahmanical tradition, however, derives the name from *Mura*, the low-caste, to which, they allege, CHANDRA-GUPTA's mother, belonged,[2] and this appears to be the origin of the current form of the name '*Maurya*.'

The Buddhistic accounts assert, as they usually do in regard to the genealogy of those kings who especially patronized Buddhism, that the dynasty of the great Buddhist king, ASOKA, was also an offshoot of *Buddha Śākya Muni's* own. Thus the Ceylonese commentary[3] states "the *Moriyan* was a branch of the *Śākyan* dynasty who were of *Ikshwaku* of the 'solar' line. Though the name of CHANDRA-GUPTA's father is not given, . . . . . . . . . it is specifically stated that hewas the last sovereign of *Moriya* of that family and lost his life with his kingdom. His queen, who was then *enceinte*, fled with her brothers to *Pāṭaliputra* (where according to this account CHANDRA-GUPTA seems to have been born) to seek protection from their relatives, the *Nandas*," and it is further stated that CHANDRA-GUPTA succeeded the last of these NANDAS on the throne there.

1 *Mahāwainso*, TURNOUR's edn., 17.
2 WILSON'S *Hindu Theatre*.
3 Pāli *Mahāvainso* (TURN.), pref. v.

The duration of this dynasty, according to the Brahmanical accounts, was 137 years, and the number of kings is variously given as nine and ten. According to the *Vishnu Purāṇa*,[1] they were (1) CHANDRA-GUPTA, (2) BINDU-SĀRA, (3) AṢOKA (VARDHANA), (4) SUYAṢAS, (5) DAṢARATHA, (6) SANGATA, (7) SĀLIṢŪKA, (8) SOMAṢARMAN, (9) SATADHANVAN, (10) BṚIHADRATHA.

Extant Buddhistic accounts do not usually extend the list beyond ASOKA's own family.

The following genealogical tree, with especial reference to ASOKA's sons and daughters, I have compiled from various sources:—

CHANDRA-GUPTA ('Vṛishala')[2]

BINDUSĀRA [or ? 'AMITROCHATES'[3] or 'NEMITA'[4]]

SUSIMA — ASOKA — MAHENDRA ('MAHINDO')

(sons of Asoka:) JALAUKA[5] — KUNĀLA — TISHYA, KUSHTANA,[6] SANGA-MITRA,[7] CHARU-MATI,[8] MAHI-PĀNA[9]

(son of Kunāla:) DASARATHA [or ? SAMPRATI].[10]

The name of the last noted, the grandson of ASOKA, has been found inscribed on one of the five rock-cut caves at *Barabar* near Gāya, which are the oldest artificial caves yet found in India, and two of them have inscriptions dated in the 12th and 19th years of PRIYADARSI, *i.e.*, ASOKA himself. The inscription of DAṢARATHA is in the same character as found in the edicts of ASOKA, and the same title is used, namely 'Beloved of the Gods' (*Devānampriya*).

---

1 WILSON's transl., IV, 186. Conf. also C. M. DUFF's *Chronology of India*, p. 325, for a comparative table.

2 A contemptuous Brahmanical title implying a *Sudra* origin. WILSON's *Hind. Theatre*, 132. For an account of him see WILFORD, *As. Researches*, V and IX, 93.

3 Greek account already quoted; also WILFORD, *As. Researches*, V, 286.

4 TĀRANĀTHA's *Tibetan History of Buddhism in India*.

5 The Kashmir Chronicle. The legends regarding him are related at some length in Book I, verses 107—152 of Dr. STEIN's edition and translation.

6 Alleged founder of Buddhist dynasty in Khoten (ROCKHILL's *Life of B.*, 236).

7 She is alleged by Ceylonese to have accompanied MAHENDRA to Ceylon (*Mahāvaṁsa*).

8 She is stated to have accompanied ASOKA to Khatmandu shrine and settled there, *Vernacular Hist. of Nepal* (WRIGHT's) p. 111.

9 *Idem.*

10 *Sampati*, according to Jain list, was the grandson and successor of ASOKA (*Parisishtaparvan*, ed. JACOBI *Sac. Bks. East.*, XXII, 290), and said to be converted to Jainism.

APPENDIX II.

# ORIGIN OF STONE BUILDING AND SCULPTURE IN INDIA.

ON this interesting question the broad fact noticed by JAMES FERGUSSON about sixty years ago[1] still holds true: that "no (stone) building is known to exist or any cave possessing any architectural character whose date can be extended back to the time when ALEXANDER THE GREAT visited India . . . . . . , that nothing that can properly be called architecture is to be found there (in India) till considerably after ALEXANDER'S time," and "that the history of art in India begins with . . . . . . the introduction of Buddhism as a State religion under ASOKA in the middle of the 3rd century B.C. . . . . . . that stone architecture commenced in India only 250 years before Christ."[2]

The only exception referred to by FERGUSSON was the so-called 'throne of *Jarasandha*' on the *Rājgir* hills. This rude tower, built of masses of unhewn stones picked up from the rocky hillsides and fitted together without mortar, was, he supposed, older than ASOKA's age, and he made the interesting observation that its form and structure "point almost undoubtedly to *Assyria* as the country from which its forms were derived, and the *Birs Nimrud* with its range of little cells on two sides seems only a gigantic model of what is here copied on a small and rude scale."[3]

Here, however, I may note that nothing has been found to prove conclusively that this tower was erected before ASOKA's epoch, or to support General CUNNINGHAM's conjecture that its stones were quarried out of the rude cavern behind it, which seems merely one of the many natural caves abounding in those hills. Nor can the adjoining rough stone-wall of the town of 'new *Rājgir*,' the stones of which also bear no marks of the chisel, be placed with confidence before ASOKA's epoch, although the town itself is said to have been founded over a century previously. Indeed, one of the chief accounts of ASOKA[4] alleges that that monarch at first resided at *Rājgir* and afterwards transferred his capital to *Pāṭaliputra*.

Similarly, too, with regard to the rock-cut inscription on the 'Elephant-cave' on the *Khandagiri-Udayagiri* hill near *Katak* in *Orissa*—this inscription, which FERGUSSON accepted as being about a century earlier than ASOKA, has since been conclusively proved to be not anterior to ASOKA's time. I have personally visited each and all of the above-mentioned objects (the tower, wall, and caves), and have carefully examined them with especial reference to this question.

Nor do the references to the alleged earlier occurrence of the word for 'bricks' in Indian literature, which were put forward by Babu Rajendralal Mitra and others[5] in trying to prove an earlier origin for stone architecture, shed any trustworthy light on the subject; for the books in question are very corrupt, having been freely altered and added to by the copyists,

---

[1] *Journ. Royal Asiatic Soc.* VIII, pp. 30, etc., 1843. *Tree and Serpent Worship, 1868. History of Indian and Eastern Architecture, 1876. Indian Archæology with especial reference to Babu Rajendralal Mitra.* By J. FERGUSSON, 1884.

[2] *Cave Temples of India,*—J. FERGUSSON and J. BURGESS, 1880, p. 29.

[3] *Id.*, 34.

[4] HIUEN TSIANG'S *Records, &c.*, see Appendix V, p. 72.

[5] *Indo-Aryans* and *Antiquities of Orissa.*

and it is even doubtful whether any of them were compiled in anything like their present form before ASOKA's epoch. Thus the *Mahābhārata* in the diverse modern versions of which the word for 'bricks' occurs is placed by MEHER as late as about the second century B.C., and the *Ramāyaṇa* still later.[1] Besides, the Indian alphabet itself has recently been proved by Dr. BÜHLER to be derived from the Phœnician.

Altogether the most trustworthy evidence available seems to lead to the conclusion that India derived its knowledge of the art of working in stone from the West, and that this event occurred probably during ASOKA's reign. The present report supplies some further evidence in this direction.

[1] Quoted through DOWSON'S *Classical Dictionary of Hindu Mythology*, p. 190.

APPENDIX III.

# LEGEND OF THE FOUNDING OF PĀTALIPUTRA.

THE place is described in the Buddhist Scriptures as being only a small village called '*Pāṭali*' at the time of Buddha's visit to it a few months before his death, and when he was reported to have prophesied its future greatness, and complimented the *Brahman* VARSHAKĀRA, the minister of King AJĀTASATRU of Magadha on his wise foresight in fortifying so important a spot.[1] It seems to have been near the site of an older town named 'The city of sweet-scented flowers,' *Kusumpura,* which probably was washed away in front part by the Ganges; for it is frequently referred to under this name, and HIUEN TSIANG states[2] regarding it that "formerly it was called *Kusumpura* . . . . . . . . . . . afterwards . . . . . . . . . . . . its name was changed to *Pāṭaliputra* (or 'The son of a *pāṭali* tree'[3])," and here the Chinese pilgrim relates the then current legend that the city was so called because its founder married the daughter of a *pāṭali* flower

A more picturesque version of the fabulous origin of this famous city, having its parallels in GRIMM's *Fairy Tales* and the *Arabian Nights,* is given in the mediæval *Ocean of the Streams of Story.*[4] According to this account a person called PUTRAKA of *Rājgir,* whose ancestors came from the Himalayas, finds in the *Vindhaya* mountains two sons of the giants disputing about their parental heritage, which consisted of a magical vase, a wizard's wand, and a pair of magic slippers. The slippers conferred the power of flying through the air to any place their wearer wished; the vase offered whatever food or riches a person desired, and whatever was written with the wand came true or was realized. By stratagem, as an arbitrator between the two disputants, PUTRAKA becomes possessed of these objects and flies away with them. They confer on him facilities for making love to the beautiful *Pāṭali,* the daughter of King MAHENDRA-VARMAN of *Ākarshikā,* and enables him to carry her off from the palace of her father. Having reached the bank of the Ganges, he there, in compliance with the request of his beloved one, by the miraculous virtue of his staff builds a city, which in honour of the princess he called *Pāṭaliputra.* He becomes a powerful monarch, is reconciled to his father-in-law, and governs all the country as far as the sea.

The Greek version of the legend gives a somewhat similar outline, omitting the more miraculous details. It states that the giant HERCULES, the founder of *Pāṭaliputra,* "begot a daughter in India whom he called '*Pandaia.*' To her he assigned that portion of India which lies southwards and extends to the sea."[5]

---

[1] *Life of the Buddha* from the Tibetan. ROCKHILL, p. 127, &c.
[2] BEAL'S *Records, ii,* 82.
[3] *Stereospermum suaveolens.*
[4] *Kathā Sarit Sāgara,* translated by C. H. TAWNEY, Calcutta, 1881, I, 14, &c. See also H. BROCKHAUS' *Foundation of Pāṭali-putra,* Liepsic, 1835, and summarized by KLAPROTH in his translation of FA HIAN'S travels.
[5] POLYÆN. *Strateg,* I, 34 ; MCCRINDLE, 168.

The town seems first to have become the capital in the reign of UDAYĀŚVA or UDĀYIN, the son[1] or grandson of King AJĀTSATRU, who was reigning at Buddha's visit, and the predecessor of NANDA whom CHĀNDRAGUPTA superseded. This name is also given as UDAYANA[2] who has a legendary history very like that of PUTRAKA in the above fairy tale. UDYANA or VATSA was the son of SAHASRĀNĪKA and grandson of S'ATĀNĪKA, who transferred the capital of Upper India from *Hāstinapur* to *Kausāmbi* S'ATĀNĪKA was the great great grandson of ARJUNA. VATSA was named UDAYANA from being educated on the Eastern or *Udaya* mountain by the sage JAMADAGNI. When arrived at maturity he was decoyed into captivity by Chandrasena, King of *Ujjayin*. He was liberated by his minister, YOGANDHARĀYAṆA, and in his escape carried off VĀSVADATTĀ, the daughter of his captor. His adventures are recorded in the RATNĀVALI and in VĀSVADATTĀ's poem and in the *Vrihat-katha*. They have been translated from the latter and published in the "Calcutta Quarterly Magazine" for June 1874.[3]

This supernatural origin ascribed to *Pāṭaliputra* and its association with the giants and Hercules appear to be based largely on the gigantic stones used by ASOKA for his buildings and monuments.

[1] The Jain list (*Parisishtaparv.* JACOBI) puts him immediately after AJĀTASATRU, and I think it is worth considering whether the intervening person in the *Pauranic* lists variously called HARSHAKA, VAINŚAKA, DASAKA and otherwise is not really the contemporary minister of AJĀTASATRU, namely, 'VARSHAKĀRA,' especially as the Jain list places his death only 60 years after that of MAHĀVIRA, who died before Buddha; and the *Purāṇas* give his reign as 23—33 years, and AJĀTASATRU'S at 25—35.

[2] *Vishnu Purāṇa.*

[3] WILSON'S *Hindu Theatre*, I, 81.

## APPENDIX IV.

# STATUES OF ASOKA'S GENII.

Two life-sized statues of ASOKA's gigantic masons were "dug out of a field near *Patna*" about 1820, and "in the same spot was a third image still unremoved, but where the spot was he could never learn."[1] Such is the record sent with these most ancient statues to the Calcutta Museum by the donor, MR. J. TYTLER. Although from the inscriptions which they bear they are amongst the oldest of Indian statues: they are of high artistic value. Their massive shoulders and powerful arms, yet dignified pose, well convey the idea of Intelligent Strength which it was the artist's object to portray. It is rather a commentary on 'Indian' Art to find that its earliest efforts were the most successful. The two statues are lightly draped from the waist downwards with a loose robe girded at the waist by a tasselled cord, and a thin scarf thrown over the left shoulder. The heavy necklets, armlets and earrings generally resemble those of the *Bharhut* sculptures, as pointed out by Dr. ANDERSON, though the art altogether is decidedly superior. The stone is a close-grained sandstone like that of ASOKA's edict-pillars, and is also like these high-polished. As one holds a fly-whisk or *chauri*, the oriental symbol of an attendant on royalty, as they were probably attendant figures at a shrine before the introduction of actual images of Buddha himself.

The inscriptions record that the statues are those of *Yakshas*,[2] that is, the fabulous *genii* to which the cyclopean masonry of ASOKA's period was afterwards ascribed.

The worship of these *Yakshas*, or 'Jak,' as they are now called, seems to have been very prevalent in Mid-India in early times. In the Tibetan version of the Buddhist Scriptures it is stated[3] that the tribal god of Buddha's tribe, the *Sâkyas*, was a *Yaksha* of the good genius type named 'the Bestower or Increaser of Gifts.'[4] Also in the same canon it is related in describing the exploits of King BIMBASĀRA of *Râjgir*, a contemporary of Buddha, that "at that time one of the gate-keepers of *Vaisâli* died and had been born again among the demons. He gave the inhabitants of *Vaisâli* the following instructions: 'As I have been born again among the demons, confer on me the position of a *Yaksha* and hang a bell round my neck. Whenever a foe to the inhabitants of *Vaisâli* appears, I will make the bell sound until he is arrested or has taken his departure.' *So they caused a Yaksha statue to be prepared* and hung a bell round its neck. Then they set it up in the gate-house provided with oblations and garlands along with dance and song and to the sound of musical instruments."[5]

---

[1] Catalogue and Hand-book of the Archæological collections in the Indian Museum, by J. ANDERSON, M.D., part I, 152.

[2] The characters are somewhat later than ASOKA's epoch and are read by Genl. CUNNINGHAM (*Rept.* XV, 3) as *Yakhe Sanatananda* (? or *Bharata*), and *Yakhe Achusatigika* (? or *Sanigika*), and a drawing of the statues are given in the same report.

[3] CSOMA DE KÖRÖ's *Analysis* in *Asiatic Researches*, XX, 300.

[4] *Gnan-spyin.*

[5] SCHIEFNER's *Tibetan Tales from the Kah-gyur*, RALSTON's trans., 81.

The *Yakshas* are minor divinities, mostly good-natured. Their chief is VAISRAVAN or the Hindu KUVERA, the god of wealth and guardian of the northern part of the world, and he was early given a prominent place in the Buddhist pantheon. *Māra* is called a *Yakhas*.[1] A list of 8 chief *Yakshas* is given in the Tibetan scripture,[2] and many of these divinities are figured and their names inscribed on the *Bharhut* Railing.[3]

Human *Yakskas* are also described in that primitive collection of Buddhist scriptures, the *Sutta Nipāta*, as reigning over various parts of the country during Buddha's day and as having conversations with Buddha and being converted by him. Thus at *Gāya* were SŪCHILOMA and KHARA, at *Ātavi* (possibly *Uren*)[4] ALAVAKA, and SĀTĀGIRA and HEMAVATA[5] are also therein mentioned. They were probably aboriginal tribesmen, and were paid local respect and afterwards semi-divine honours, as seems latterly to have been the case with the aboriginal tribesmen classed as *Naga* and mixed up with mythological beings of the same name.

---

1 *Sacred B. E.*, X, 2, 72.
2 *Gyut* Pa (13th Vol.) leaf 117—134 (CSOMA 517).
3 *Yaksha Supravasu* (*Supāvaso*) evidently is figured on the S. E. quadrant of the circle.—ANDERSON *Catal.*
4 See my art. *Journal* Asiatic Socy. (Bengal), part I, No. 1, 1892.
5 *Sacred B. E.*, X, pt. 2, 26, 29, 45.

APPENDIX V.

# DESCRIPTIONS OF PĀṬALIPUTRA FROM THE CHINESE

## (*A.*) BY FA HIAN.

(*About 400A.D.*)

---

THE Chinese Buddhist pilgrim FA HIAN travelled in India for fifteen years about 399—414A.D. in search of Buddhist scriptures. The following translation of his narrative, from Professor J. Legge's version[1] annotated from that of Professor Beal,[2] is appended for convenience of reference:—

"Four *yojanas* on from this place (*Vaisāli*) to the east brought the travellers to the confluence of the five rivers. * * * * Having crossed the river and descended south for a *Yojana* (the travellers) came to the town of *Pāṭaliputra*, in the kingdom of *Magadha*, the city where King ASOKA ruled. The royal palace and halls in the midst of the city, which exist now as of old, were all made by spirits[3] which he employed, and which piled up the stones, reared the walls and gates, and executed the elegant carving and inlaid sculpture-work,—in a way which no human hands of this world could accomplish.

King ASOKA had a younger brother who had attained to be an *Arhat*, and resided on *Gridhra-kûṭa* hill, finding his delight in solitude and quiet. The King, who sincerely reverenced him, wished and begged him (to come and live) in his family,[4] where he could supply all his wants. The other, however, through his delight in the stillness of the mountain, was unwilling to accept the invitation, on which the King said to him, 'Only accept my invitation, and I will make a hill for you inside the city.' Accordingly, he provided the materials of a feast, called to him the spirits,[5] and announced to them, 'To-morrow you will all receive my invitation; but as there are no mats for you to sit on, let each one bring (his own seat).' Next day the spirits came, each one bringing with him a great rock, (like) a wall, four or five paces square, (for a seat). When their sitting was over, the King made them form a hill with the large stones piled on one another, and also at the foot of the hill, with five large square stones, to make an apartment, which might be more than thirty cubits long, twenty cubits wide, and more than ten cubits high.[6]

In this city there had resided a great Brahman, named RĀDHA-SVAMI, a professor of the *Mahāyāna*, of clear discernment and much wisdom, who

---

[1] *Records of Buddhistic Kingdoms*, &c., Oxford, 1886.

[2] *Buddhist Records* of the Western World, transld. from the Chinese by S. BEAL, I. lv, *et seq.*, which here will be referred to as 'B.'

[3] Genii—B.

[4] House—B.

[5] Genii—B.

[6] The standard specified is a *chang*, which LEGGE converts at the rate of about 15 cubits but BEAL at about 12 feet, thus BEAL gives these measurements as "about 35 feet in length 22 feet in breadth, in height 11 feet or 50."

understood everything, living by himself in spotless purity.[1] The King of the country honoured and reverenced him, and served him as his teacher. If he went to inquire for and greet him, the King did not presume to sit down alongside of him; and if, in his love and reverence, he took hold of his hand, as soon as he let it go, the Brahman made haste to pour water on it and wash it. He might be more than fifty years old, and all the Kingdom looked up to him. By means of this one man, the Law of Buddha was widely made known, and the followers of other doctrines did not find it in their power to persecute the body of monks in any way.

By the side of the *tope* (tower) of ASOKA. there has been made a *mahâyāna* monastery, very grand and beautiful; there is also a *hînayāna* one; the two together containing six hundred or seven hundred monks. The rules of demeanour and the scholastic arrangements in them are worthy of observation.

*Shamans* (ascetics) of the highest virtue from all quarters, and students, inquirers wishing to find out truth and the grounds of it, all resort to these monasteries. There also resides in this monastery a Brahman teacher, whose name also is MAÑJUSRI, whom the *shamans* of greatest virtue in the kingdom, and the *mahāyāna Bhikshus* honour and look up to.

The cities and towns of this country are the greatest of all in the Middle kingdom. The inhabitants are rich and prosperous, and vie with one another in the practice of benevolence and righteousness. Every year on the eighth day of the second month they celebrate a procession of images. They make a four-wheeled car, and on it erect a structure of five storeys by means of bamboos tied together. This is supported by a king-post with poles and lances slanting from it, and is rather more than twenty cubits high, having the shape of a tope. White and silk-like cloth of hair is wrapped all round it, which is then painted in various colours. They make figures of devas, with gold, silver, and lapis lazuli grandly blended and having silken streamers and canopies hung out over them. On the four sides are niches, with a Buddha seated in each, and a *Bodhisattva* standing in attendance on him. There may be twenty cars, all grand and imposing, but each one different from the others. On the day mentioned, the monks and laity within the borders all come together; they have singers and skilful musicians; they pay their devotions with flowers and incense. The Brahmans come and invite the Buddhas to enter the city. These do so in order, and remain two nights in it. All through the night they keep lamps burning, have skilful music, and present offerings. This is the practice in all the other kingdoms as well. The heads of the *Vaiśya* families in them establish in the cities houses for dispensing charity and medicines. All the poor and destitute in the country, orphans, widowers, and childless men, maimed people and cripples, and all who are diseased, go to those houses and are provided with every kind of help, and doctors examine their diseases. They get the food and medicines which their cases require, and are made to feel at ease; and when they are better, they go away themselves.

When King ASOKA destroyed the seven *topes* (intending) to make eighty-four thousand, the first which he made was the great *tope*, more than three *le* to the south of this city. In front of this there is a foot-print of Buddha,

1 Silent meditation—B.

where a *vihāra* has been built. The door of it faces the north, and on the south of it there is a stone pillar, fourteen or fifteen cubits in circumference, and more than thirty cubits high, on which there is an inscription, saying, 'ASOKA gave the (whole of)[1] *Jambudvīpa* (India) to the general body of all the monks, and then redeemed it from them with money. This he did three times.' North from the *tope* 300 or 400 paces, King ASOKA built the city of *Ne-le.*[2] In it there is a stone pillar, which also is more than thirty feet high, with a lion on the top of it. On the pillar there is an inscription recording the things which led to the building of *Ne-le*, with the number of the year, the day, and the month.

* * * * * *

"From *Vârânasî* (the travellers) went back east to *Pāṭaliputra.* FA-HIAN's original object had been to search for (copies of) the *Vinaya.* In the various kingdoms of North India, however, he had found one master transmitting orally (the rules) to another, but no written copies which he could transcribe. He had therefore travelled far and come on to Central India. Here, in the *mahāyāna* monastery, he found a copy of the *Vinaya*, containing the *Mahāsânghika* rules,—those which were observed in the first Great Council, while Buddha was still in the world. The original copy was handed down in the *Jetavana-vihâra.* As to the other eighteen schools, each one has the views and decisions of its own masters. Those agree (with this) in the general meaning, but they have small and trivial differences, as when one opens and another shuts. This copy (of the rules), however, is the most complete, with the fullest explanations.

He further got a transcript of the rules in six or seven thousand *gāthas*, being the *sarvāstivâdâh* rules,—those which are observed by the communities of monks in the land of *Ts'in*, which also have all been handed down orally from master to master without being committed to writing. In the community here, moreover, he got the *Saṁyuktâbhi-dharma-hridaya* (*sâstra*) containing about six or seven thousand gâthas; he also got a *Sûtra* of 2,500 gâthas; one chapter of the *Parinirvâna-vaipulya sûtra*, of about 5,000 *gāthas* and the *Mahâsânghikâh Abhidharma.*

In consequence (of this success in his quest) FA-HIAN stayed here for three years, learning Sanskrit books and the Sanskrit speech, and writing out the *Vinaya* rules.

## (*B.*) BY HIUEN TSIANG.

(*About 635 A.D.*)

IN the following extract from the narrative of the Chinese Buddhist pilgrim Hiuen Tsiang, taken from BEAL's translation[3] and annotated, also from JULIEN's,[4] I have for the convenience of the reader inserted here references to my plan of the site as given at page 12.

---

[1] B.

[2] 'Ni-li' is the more usual form as given by KLAPROTH and BEAL: and as remarked by Genl. CUNNINGHAM, the present name of the land in which *Kumrāhar* is situated is *Nirand-pur* which possibly preserves the old name.

[3] *Op. cit.* [4] *Op. cit.*

I. "To the south of the river Ganges (in Magadha), there is an old city about 70 *li* (= about 12 miles) round. Although it has been long deserted, its foundation-walls still survive. Formerly when men's lives were incalculably long, it was called *Kusumpura*, so called because the palace of the King had many flowers. Afterwards when men's age reached several thousands of years, then its name was changed to *Pāṭaliputra*, [and here HIUEN TSIANG gives in detail the current legend as to why the city was called 'The son of the *Pāṭali* tree' (*Stereospermum suaveolens*) owing to the founder of the city having married the daughter of (a spirit-inhabiting) a *Pāṭali* tree, or the flower of that tree—see also page 67].

II. "To the north of the old palace of the King (4 on plan) is a stone pillar (2 on plan) several tens of feet high: this is the place where ASOKA Rāja made 'a hell.' In the hundreth year after the *Nirvāna* of Tathāgatha there was a king called Asoka (or the sorrowless), who was the great-grandson of BIMBASĀRA Rāja. He changed his capital from *Rājagṛha* to *Pāṭali*, and built an outside rampart to surround the old city. Since then many generations have passed, and there remain only the old foundation walls. The *sanghārāmas*, *deva* temples, and *stupas* which lie in ruins may be counted by hundreds. There are only two or three remaining entire. To the north of the old palace and bordering on the Ganges river there is a little town, which contains about 1,000 houses. At first when ASOKA Rāja ascended the throne, he exercised a most cruel tyranny: he constituted a hell for the purpose of torturing living creatures. [Here follows the 'Hell' legend which is given at greater length by FA HIAN;[1] and in both versions it is made the scene of ASOKA's conversion to Buddhism, through seeing the miraculous preservation there of a *sramana* or Buddhist monk who had been cast into a fiery furnace.]

III. "To the south of the earth prison (the hell) and not far off is a *stupa* (5 on plan). Its foundation walls are sunk, and it is in a leaning ruinous condition. There remains, however, the crowning jewel of the cupola. This is made of carved stone, and has a surrounding balustrade. This was the first of the 84,000 (stupas). ASOKA Rāja erected it by the power of man in the middle of his royal precinct. It contains a *ching* of relics of the *Tathāgatha* (*i.e.*, the Buddha). Spiritual indications constantly manifest themselves, and a divine light is shed around it from time to time.

IV. "By the side of the *stupa*, and not far from it in a *vihara* is a great stone (7 on plan) on which Tathāgatha walked. There is still the impression of both his feet on it, about 18 inches long and 6 inches broad; both the right and left impress have the circle sign, and the ten toes are all fringed with figures of flowers (or flower scrolls), and forms of fishes which glisten brightly in the morning light. In old time *Tathāgotha* being about to attain *Nirvāṇa* was going northward to *Kusinagara*, when turning round to the south and looking back at Magadha, he stood upon this stone and said to Ananda: 'Now, for the very last time, I leave this foot impression, being about to attain Nirvāna' and looking at Magadha: 'A hundred years hence there shall be a King ASOKA; he shall build here his capital and establish his court and he shall protect the three treasures and command the genii.' When ASOKA had ascended the

[1] *Op. cit.*, see p. 73.

throne he changed his capital and built this town; he enclosed the stone with the impression, and as it was near the royal precinct, he paid it constant personal worship. Afterwards the kings of the neighbourhood wished to carry it off to their own country; but although the stone is not large, they could not move it at all. Lately Śaśāṅka Rajā, when he was overthrowing and destroying the law of Buddha, forthwith came to the place where the stone is for the purpose of destroying the sacred marks. Having broken it into pieces, it came whole again, and the ornamental figures as before. Then he flung it into the river Ganges, but it came back to its old place.

V. "By the side of the stone is a stupa (8 on plan) which marks the place where the four past Buddhas walked and sat down, the traces of which still remain.

VI. "By the side of the *vihara* (7 on plan) which contains the traces of Buddha, and not far from it is a great stone pillar, about 30 feet high, with a mutilated inscription on it. This, however, is part of it, *viz.*, Asoka Rāja with a firm principle of faith has thrice bestowed *Jambudwipa* (India) as a religious offering on Buddha, the *Dharma* (the law) and the Assembly, and thrice he had redeemed it with his jewels and treasures, 'and this is the record thereof.'

VII. "To the north of the old palace is a large stone-house (1 on plan). It looks outside like a great mountain, and within it is many tens of feet wide. This is the house which Asoka Rāja commanded the genii to build for his brother who had become a recluse * * * * * * a half-brother called Mahendra, who was born of a noble tribe * * * * * * * * The King said: 'If you wish to subdue your heart *in quiet* you have no need to live in the mountain fastness. To meet your wishes I shall construct you a dwelling.' Accordingly he summoned the genii to his presence. * * * * * * * * The genii having received the order, before the day was over finished the task. Asoka Rāja then himself went to invite his brother to fix his abode in this mountain cell.

VIII. "To the north of the old palace and to the south of the hill is a great stone with a hollow trough in it (3 on plan) Asoka Rāja commissioned the genii as workmen to make this hollow (vase) to use for the food which he gave to the priests when he invited them to eat.

IX. "To the south-west of the old palace there is a little mountain (9 on plan). In the crags and surrounding valleys there are several tens of stone dwellings which Asoka Rāja made for Upagupta and other *arhats* by the intervention of the genii.

X. "By the side of it is an old tower, the ruins of which are a mass of heaped up stones. There is also a pond (10 on plan), the gentle ripples of which play over its surface as pure as a mirror. The people far and near call it '*the sacred water*.' If any one drinks thereof or washes in it, the defilement of his sins is washed away and destroyed.

XI. "To the south-west of the mountain is a collection of five stupas (11 on plan). The foundations are lofty, but ruinous; what remains, however, is a good height. At a distance they look like little hills. Each of them is several tens of paces in front. Men in after-days tried to build on the top of these little stupas. The records of India state: 'In old time when Asoka Rāja built the 84,000 stupas, there were still remaining five measures of relics.' Therefore he erected *with exceptional grandeur* five other stupas remarkable for their miraculous exhibition with a view to indicate the five-fold spiritual body of Tathāgatha. Some disciples of little faith talking together argued thus: 'In old time NANDA Rāja built these five (stupas) as treasure places for his wealth. In consequence of this gossip in after-time a king of insincere faith, and excited by his covetousness, came with his followers to dig (the stupas). It is said, moreover (*i.e.*, in the Indian records), with respect to the gossip of the priests there has been some doubt expressed, but we believe it to be true according to the old tradition.'

XII. "To the south-east of the old city [N. B.—*not* palace] there is the *Sanghārāma* called *Kukkutārāma* (14 on plan) which was built by ASOKA Rāja when he first became a believer in the religion of Buddha. It was a sort of first fruit and *a pattern of majestic construction.* He gathered there a thousand priests. This building has long been in ruins, but the foundation walls are still preserved.

XIII. "By the side of the *Sangharama* is a great *stūpa* (15 on plan) called '*Amalaka*,' which is the name of a fruit used as a medicine in India. King ASOKA having fallen sick and lingering for a long time felt that he would not recover, and so desired to offer all his possessions so as to crown his religious merit. The minister, who was carrying on the government, was unwilling to comply with this wish * * * * [Then Asoka bewailing his lot exclaimed :] 'The empire is no longer mine, this half fruit alone is left. * * * * Take this half fruit and offer it in The-Garden-of-the-Cock (monastery) to the priests.' * * * * The *Sthavira* in the midst of the priests spoke in reply: 'ASOKA Rāja by his former deeds may hope to recover. * * * This offering of half a fruit will secure the King an extension of life.' The King having recovered from his sickness gave large offerings to the priests * * * and he erected this stupa as a mark of gratitude for his prolonged life.

XIV. "To the north-west of the *Amalaka* stupa in the middle of an old *Sanghārāma* is a *stūpa* (16 on plan); it is called 'establishing the sound of the *ghanta*' [and a long account is given of how the name was bestowed owing to the Buddhist monk DEVA, a pupil of the great NAGARJUNA, striking the *ghanta* or gong as a challenge to the heretics, *i.e.*, Jains.] * * * Then the King assembled the men of learning (the Buddhists), and said by way of decree 'whoever is defeated shall die as proof of his inferiority.' * * * In less than one hour he (DEVA) refuted the sectaries, and the King and his ministers being satisfied raised this venerable monument in honour of his extreme virtue.

XV. "To the north of the stupa built where the *ghanta* was sounded is an old foundation (17 on plan). This was the dwelling place of a Brahman that was inspired by demons. * * * Officers and people looked on him as a saint [until he was signally defeated in argument by the *Bodhisattwa* AŚVA GHOSHA]"

APPENDIX VI.

# LEGEND OF ASOKA'S HELL.

IN addition to the details supplied in the foregoing account of HIUEN TSIANG, the following version of the legend is related by FA HIAN.[1] "When King AŚOKA, in a former birth, was a little boy and playing on the road, he met KAŚYAPA[2] Buddha walking. (The stranger) begged food, and the boy pleasantly took a handful of earth and gave it to him. The Buddha took the earth, and returned it to the ground on which he was walking; bue because of this (the boy) received the recompense of becoming a king of tht iron wheel, to rule over *Jambudvipa* (*India*). (Once) when he was making a judicial tour of inspection through *Jambudvipa*, he saw, between the iron circuit of the two hills, a *naraka* (hell) for the punishment of wicked men. Having thereupon asked his ministers what sort of a thing it was, they replied, 'It belongs to *Yama*, king of demons, for punishing wicked people.' The king thought within himself:—'(even) the king of demons is able to make a *naraka* in which to deal with wicked men; why should not I, who am the lord of men, make a *naraka* in which to deal with wicked men?' He forthwith asked his ministers who could make for him a *naraka* and preside over the punishment of wicked people in it.

"They replied that it was only a man of extreme wickedness who could make it; and the king thereupon sent officers to seek everywhere for (such) a bad man; and they saw by the side of a pond a man tall and strong, with a black countenance, yellow hair, and green eyes, hooking up the fish with his feet, while he called to him birds and beasts, and, when they came, then shot and killed them, so that not one escaped. Having got this man, they took him to the king, who secretly charged him, 'You must make a square enclosure with high walls. Plant in it all kinds of flowers and fruits; make good ponds in it for bathing; make it grand and imposing in every way, so that men shall look to it with thirsting desire; make its gates strong and sure; and when any one enters, instantly seize him and punish him as a sinner, not allowing him to get out. Even if I should enter, punish me as a sinner in the same way, and do not let me go. I now appoint you master of that *naraka*.'

"Soon after this a *bhikshu*, pursuing his regular course of begging his food, entered the gate (of the place). When the lictors of the *naraka* saw him, they were about to subject him to their tortures; but he, frightened, begged them to allow him a moment in which to eat his midday meal. Immediately after there came in another man, whom they thrust into a mortar and pounded till a red froth overflowed. As the *bhikshu* looked on, there came to him the thought of the impermanence, the painful suffering and inanity of this body, and how it is but as a bubble and as foam; and instantly he attained to *Arhatship*. Immediately after, the lictors seized him, and threw him into a cauldron of boiling water. There was a look of joyful satisfaction, however, in the *bhikshu's* countenance. The fire was extinguished

---

[1] *loc. cit* Chapter XXXII.

[2] *Sâkya*—BEAL, and LEGGE notes that the Chinese text has '*Sâkya*,' but he prefers a Corean manuscript which gives *Kasyapa*.

and the water became cold. In the middle (of the cauldron) there rose up a lotus flower, with the *bhikshu* seated on it! The lictors at once went and reported to the king that there was a marvellous occurrence in the *naraka* and wished him to go and see it; but the King said, 'I formerly made such an agreement that now I dare not go (to the place).' The lictors said, 'This is not a small matter. Your majesty ought to go quickly. Let your former agreement be altered.' The King thereupon followed them, and entered (the *naraka*), when the *bhikshu* preached the Law to him, and he believed, and was made free. Forthwith he demolished the *naraka*, and repented of all the evil which he had formerly done. From this time he believed in and honoured the Three Precious Ones."

APPENDIX VII.

MR. C. R. WILSON'S

# REPORT ON THE EXCAVATIONS AT CHHOTI PAHARI IN 1899.

THESE excavations took place in March and April, 1899. They were instituted by Major L. A. Waddell, I.M.S., and they were made under the immediate supervision of the Surveyor to the Bankipore District Board, Ahmad Husain. I went down almost every day to the excavations, reported almost every day to Dr. Waddell, and tried, as far as I could, to see that the excavations were properly conducted.

2. Chhoti Pahari is a mound of brick work, a little more than a mile to the south of old Kumrahar and the East Indian Railway, and about the same distance to the south-east from a very ancient well called the Agam Kuā. Hiuen Tsiang in his account of the ruins of Asoka's capital describes a hell for tormenting living creatures which Asoka Rājā was said to have made when he first ascended the throne. "To the south of the earth prison," he says, "and not far off is a stupa. Its foundation-walls are sunk, and it is in a leaning ruinous condition. There remains, however, the crowning jewel of the cupola. This is made of carved stone and has a surrounding balustrade. This was the first of the 84,000 (*stūpas*). Asoka Rājā erected it by the power of man in the middle of his royal precinct. It contains a *ching* of relics of the Tathāgatha. Spiritual indications constantly manifest themselves, and a divine light is shed around it from time to time."[1] This was the first *stupa* erected by Asoka. South of it was a *vihar* of Buddha's foot-prints with another *stupa*, and south of this *vihar* was the Jambudwipa pillar.

3. On the assumption that the Agam Kuá was the site where Hiuen Tsiang saw the earth prison, Chhoti Pahari would probably be the site of the first Asoka's stūpa. Dr. Waddell hoped to verify this assumption by finding the centre of the stupa and the *ching* of relics mentioned by the Chinese pilgrim. The excavations were conducted for this purpose. It is unfortunate that Dr. Waddell could not have watched over them in person. I did my best, but I regret to say that I was unable to discover the centre of this supposed *stūpa.*

4. The mound is a mass of brick-work covered with earth in which are a few graves, or supposed graves. The road runs on the west side, and on the north is the village standing on high ground. The mound is more than 100 feet in diameter. The highest point was to the north-west, and on it was placed a lingam. The centre of the mound was cut through by a deep excavation from south-east to north-west. This excavation, I understand, was made by the orders of Mr. C. J. O'Donnell, C.S., under the supervision of a *kanungo*, who, after destroying large masses of brick-work, reported that he could find nothing. Ahmad Husain, however, said that he remembered

[1] *Discovery of Asoka's Classic Capital of Pātal putra* by L. A. Waddell, 1892, p. 4.

seeing lines of bricks converging to a point as if they radiated from a centre. In many *stūpas*, which have been excavated, the middle is marked by a well, or pipe, around which the bricks are arranged concentrically, and Dr. Waddell hoped to find similar indications of the centre in the present case.

5. In order to determine the centre of the stūpa, Ahmad Husain was directed to excavate six cuts, or trenches, at different points on the probable circumference, and also to clear away all the earth and rubbish which covered the brick-work and filled the great central excavations, where he said he had seen the bricks radiating. After giving these instructions at the beginning of March, Dr. Waddell was obliged to return to Calcutta and left me to watch over the work.

6. By the 21st March, after working for about a week, remains of brick-work were found in the north-east, east and south-west cuts; and assuming that these indicated the circumference of the stūpa, I calculated that its diameter was about 106 feet, and that its centre must be somewhere in the great mass of brick-work to the north of the kanungo's excavation. I am, however, sorry to say that no solid brick-work was to be found in any of the cuts to the south, nor could we find any point in the central portions of the brick-work from which the bricks radiated.

7. During the weeks which followed I extended the cuts. In particular I tried to excavate all the earth between the brick-work found in the north-east cut and that found in the east cut so as to expose an arc of the stūpa's circumference. The results were only more and more confusing. Masses of brick work were constantly uncovered to the east of the mound, but whether they belonged to the stūpa or to other buildings it was impossible to say. Everywhere the brick-work was so cut about and mutilated that no clear outlines or contours could be made out. The same may be said of the excavations to the south-west. Due south we never could find any brick-work at all. I must add that the excavations had to be carried to great depths below the surface, so that in more than one case the cuts fell in, and in fact I had not time to excavate the whole of the site to the east of the mound, or perhaps some definite results would have been reached.

8. Coming now to the central portions of the mound, I regret to say that I found them equally confusing. The whole of the old deep excavation was cleared. But no concentric arrangement of bricks indicating a central pipe or well could be discovered. I also carefully examined the mass of brick-work to the north of the old excavation in which I was disposed to look for the centre, especially as I could discover no brick-work to the south. The uneven portions of the brick-work were removed so as to give a fairly level surface of brick which was carefully washed and swept; but though this was done several times, we never could find any concentric arrangement of bricks.

9. The bricks are about one foot square and two and-a-half inches thick. Rice straw has been used to stiffen the clay after the manner of the Asoka period. The brick-work everywhere appears quite solid, and is laid in courses generally parallel. Sometimes two lines of brick meet at a slight angle, and from this circumstance we have been more than once deceived into supposing that we were coming upon the concentric arrangement. But upon clearing the brick-work further it always turned out that this inclination of the two lines of bricks to each other was purely accidental. On removing the bricks layer by layer we generally found that the courses of

bricks were laced across each other. Thus if in one course the lines of bricks ran from north-west to south-east, in the next course they ran from north-east to south-west.

10. At one time in the course of the excavation of the brick-work I thought that I had come upon certain indications of the centre. By the 31st March I had caused a number of courses of the brick-work to be carefully removed, and proceeded to examine the course or layer now uncovered. The mud was scraped away and the brick-work swept and washed. I then saw that there was one brick sticking up in the middle of the brick-work, which did not form any part of the lines of the bricks, but which was lying in a cavity made for it in the brick-work, so that its four sides faced four cardinal points. It was clear that it had been intentionally placed in this position, and I hoped that it indicated the centre of the stūpa. Therefore before moving it I had its position accurately fixed by means of four brick columns built outside the mound determining two lines established by the theodolite, the intersection of which was at the centre of the brick. I also had a photograph taken of the brick-work, and brought one of the masters of the Bihar School of Engineering, Babu Kanhya Lall, to make a survey of the excavations as they then stood.

11. On Monday, the 3rd April, I began to remove the brick-work, but was much disappointed. On removing the projecting brick another was found under it of the same size and in the same position, and under this three similar bricks. Then the formation ceased, and the brick-work again became solid and regular.

12. Assuming that these five bricks had been set up as a mark to indicate the whereabouts of the centre, I had a cutting opened beginning at this point and extending northwards for about three or four feet. This cutting showed nothing except that the brick-work was looser towards the north and the mud damp which the workmen thought indicated the nearness of a well in the brick work. I then opened one or two places in the brick-work to the north-west of the point marked by the five bricks to see if I could get at any well or opening. But these attempts failed.

13. Lastly, giving up any attempt to find a concentric arrangement of bricks, I tried to infer the position of the centre from the slope of the brick-work. The brick-work platform on which we were working was not level, but sloped up to the north and west; in fact it seemed as if the highest point of the stūpa was covered by the lingam. On the 10th April the lingam was removed and all the earth swept away, and the brick-work carefully examined. I made several attempts to determine the slopes of the different masses of brick-work, and before leaving for England on Wednesday, the 19th, I ordered a well to be sunk at a point near where the lingam had stood and another well at the point marked by the five bricks. Neither of these I learn from Ahmad Husain has had any result.

14. On the whole, I am of opinion that the mound is a *stūpa*—probably the first *stūpa* of Asoka, though in spite of all my efforts I have not been able to determine the centre. It may be that the middle portions of the brick-work have already been cut away, and that the only method now left of determining the nature of these remains is by means of extensive excavations to the east and the south.

PATNA COLLEGE,
*The 16th November 1899.*

C. R. WILSON

## APPENDIX VIII.

# IDENTITY OF UPAGUPTA, THE HIGH PRIEST OF ASOKA WITH 'MOGALLIPUTTA TISSO.'[1]

IN a former article on Upagupta as the High-priest of ASOKA,[2] I suggested that this celebrated monk, who is frequently mentioned in the Sanskrit, Chinese and Tibetan accounts of Buddhism in India, was probably identical with Moggaliputta Tisso, the priest of Asoka according to the Ceylonese Pāli tradition, which latter however knows not the name of Upagupta, just as Moggaliputta Tisso is unknown to the former.

Further examination confirms this view of their identity. Indeed, the fragmentary accounts of these two individuals, as preserved in the leading Sanskrit and Ceylon texts on ASOKA, namely, the Sanskritic *Açōkāvadāna* and the Pāli *Mahāvaṁsa*, display such a close agreement in their descriptions, and especially in respect to the detailed circumstances of the visit of these monks to ASOKA, as to leave little doubt that they refer to one and the same person. This agreement is all the more remarkable, as these two books are considered to be derived from entirely independent sources. The *Açokāvadāna* appears to have existed in India before 317–420 A.D., when a translation from it seems to have been made into Chinese.[3] The portion of the Mahāvaṁsa in question is believed to date from about the middle of the 5th century A.D.[4]

To exhibit this agreement, I here arrange extracts from these two respective books in parallel columns:—

| ASOKĀVADĀNA.[5] | MAHĀVAMSA.[6] |
|---|---|
| *He is likened to Buddha.* | |
| "The glorious Upagupta . . . the chief amongst the interpreters of the Law, and a veritable Buddha, without the external signs . . . he will fill the *rôle* of a Buddha," p. 337. | "The illuminator of the Religion of the Jina (Buddha), the Thero, son of Moggali . . . who has heard his eloquence without considering it the eloquence of the supreme Buddha himself," pp. 33 and 71. |
| *His origin.* | |
| Upagupta was the son of a seller of perfume in Benares, p. 336.[7] | Moggaliputta Tisso was in his former existence seller of honey in Benares, p. 25.[8] |

[1] Reproduced with addition from the *Proceedings* of the Asiatic Society (Bengal), June 1899.

[2] *J. A. S. B.*, Vol. LXVI, pt. I, 1897, pp. 76 *et seq.*

[3] Bunyiu Nanjio's *Catalogue of Buddhist Tripiṭaka*, p. 300, No. 1344. But the version quoted in this article is from the Divyāvadāna as translated by Burnouf in his *Introduction a l'historie du Buddhisme Indien.*

[4] Turnour's *Mahāvaṁsa*, p. xxx. Max Müller's *Sacred Books of the East*, X, p. 13.

[5] The extracts are taken from the second edition of Burnouf's Indian Buddhism already quoted.

[6] The extracts are from Turnour's translation.

[7] *Vide* my article, *J. A. S.·B.*, p. 78.

[8] Mr. Turnour identifies this Tisso as Açoka's young brother DEVĀNAṀPIYO TISSO apparently for the reason that the name is mentioned in juxtaposition with Açoka and his wife, but it follows the name of the other great monk of Pāṭaliputra 'Nigrodho,' and the text of the Mahāvāṁsa here is evidently very involved and corrupt.

| | |
|---|---|
| *His ordination.* | |
| Upagupta was converted by Yaças or Yashka (a pupil of Sonaka)[1] who was for a time the great Sthavira at the Kukkuṭārāma monastery at Pāṭaliputra, pp. 336, 337. | Moggaliputta Tisso was taught by a pupil of Sonaka (a pupil of 'Dāsako') who was the great Thero (Sthavira) at the Kukkuṭārāma monastery of Pāṭaliputra, pp. 28 and 30. |
| *His precocity.* | |
| "He attained *Arhatship* of an exceptionally high order within three years of entering the Buddhist order,[2] becoming "like the sun shining the light of knowledge over the ruined universe," p. 339. | "This superlatively-gifted person having attained that qualification in a short time arrived at the sanctification of Sotāpatti . . . and ultimately he was elevated to a Thero . . . and became as celebrated as the sun and moon," p. 32. |
| *His hermitage.* | |
| He sojourned "in compassion for the world" (p. 338) "on the mountain Urumuṇḍa" beyond Mathurā (towards the source of Jumna and Ganges rivers), 'the first of all spots favourable for mental calm,'" p. 337. | "He sojourned for seven years in solitude in pious meditation at the 'Ahoganga'[3] mountain (beyond the Ganges) towards the source of the river," p. 39. |
| *Epoch of his visit to Asoka.* | |
| This event is placed after Asoka's conversion, p. 339. | This event is placed after Asoka's conversion, pp. 26, 34, 35. |
| *Circumstances under which invited.* | |
| "The King Asoka proceeded to the Kukkuṭa monastery at (Pāṭaliputra) and there taking the place of honour, said with hands joined in respect: 'Is there any other person, &c., &c.?' Then Yaças the Sthavira of the assembly replied thus: 'Yes, O great King! there exists one . . . the son of Gupta . . . Upagupta,'" p. 336. | "The great king Dhammāsoko . . . repairing to the chief (Buddhist) temple (of Pāṭali-putra)[4] . . . enquired of the priesthood—'Is there or is there not any priest of sufficient authority who alleviating my doubts can restore me the comforts of Religion?' The priesthood replied to the sovereign: 'O warrior king! the *Thero* Tisso, the son of Moggali, is such a person,'" p. 40. |
| *Mode of invitation—Asoka alters this on advice of his ministers, and sends a simple message.* | |
| "The king having been informed convoked a crowd of his ministers and said . . . 'I will myself go to see the Sthavira' . . . But the ministers replied, 'Sir! it is (only) necessary to send a messenger . . . the sage . . . will certainly come himself,'" p. 338. | "On that very day in order that the Thero might be brought on his invitation the (Asoka) despatched four Theras each attended by one thousand priests, &c. . . ." But the saint refuses to come, and so again when double the number are sent, then "The king enquired 'what can the cause be that the Thero doe not come.'" The priests informed him thus:—'Illustrious monarch! on sending him this message: 'Lord! vouchsafe to extend thy aid to restore me to the faith—the Thero will come,'" p. 40. |
| *Asoka arranges a Boat service to bring the Monk.* | |
| "Asoka, thinking that the Sthavira Upagupta will come by water, established boats all the way between Mathurā and Pāṭaliputra," p. 338. | "He (Asoka) thus instructed: 'The Thero (Sthavira) on account of his great age will not be disposed to mount a conveyance, do ye therefore transport the Thero in a vessel by the river,'" p. 40. |

[1] Rockhill's *Life of Buddha* from the Tibetan, p. 173.

[2] *Vide* my art. above cited, p. 78.

[3] Ahoganga hill is also made the hermitage of Sambhota Sānavāsin at the time of the 2nd Council (of Vaisali) [Mahavaṁsa] while Sambhūta's hermitage was in Mahesmati near Mathura according to the Indian authorities (Kern *Ind. Budd.*, 106) and Tibetan (Rockhill *Life of B.* 176).

[4] The Mahāvaṁsa, p. 39, says this temple was the Asokārāma.

*Acceptance of Invitation.*

"Then Upagupta to show his benevolence to king Asoka embarking . . . arrived at the town of Pāṭaliputra," p. 338.

"He (Moggaliputto Tisso) in the very act of hearing the message rose. They conveyed the Thero in a vessel," p. 40.

*Asoka advances to meet him.*

"The king advanced to meet the Sthavira Upagupta," p. 339.

"The king went out to meet him," p. 40.

*Asoka himself carries the Sage ashore.*

"(Asoka) descending from his elephant, he walked across the river-bank and fixing one foot on the bank, he placed the other on board the boat and taking in his arms the Sthavira Upagupta he transported him to the ground," p. 339.

"The monarch (proceeding) till the water reached his knees, with the profoundest respect offered the support of his right shoulder to the disembarking Thero. The benevolent Thero (Sthavira) . . . accepting the proferred right arm of the sovereign, disembarked from the vessel," p. 41.

*Conducts him to the Palace.*

"The king having then introduced in great pomp the Sthavira Upagupta into his royal abode," p. 340.

"The king conducting the Thero to the pleasure-garden *Rativaddhana*," p. 41.

*Massages(?) his limbs and seats him.*

"He (Asoka) took him betwen his arms and seated him on the seat which he had fixed. The body of the Sthavira Upagupta was refined and soft, soft as cotton wool. The king perceiving this said.—'Noble creature, thy limbs are soft as cotton, soft as the silk of Benares, but I unfortunate being, my limbs are rude and my body rough to the touch!'" p. 340.

"Bathing his feet and anointing them (Asoka) caused him to be seated," p. 41.

*Asoka asks for a miracle.*

At this meeting none are asked, as in the Mahāvaṁsa, but they were afterwards asked in somewhat the same words, pp. 341—345.

"The sovereign with the view of trying the supernatural power of the Thero said to him 'Lord, I am desirous of witnessing a miracle, . . . The Thero, manifested this miracle to him who was there seated," p. 41.

*They visit the Bodhi-tree at Gayā together.*

"Then the King (Asoka) equipped with an army of the four bodies of troops took perfumes, flowers and garlands and set out in company with the Sthavira Upagupta . . . the Sthavira Upagupta having led the king close to the Bodhi-tree, extending his hand said to him, 'Here, O great king, the Bodhi-sattva . . . attained the state of the completely perfect Buddha,'" p. 345.

"The king (Asoka) inquired (of) . . . the chief priest, the son of Moggali . . . The lord of the land hearing this reply ordered the road to the Bodhi-tree to be swept and perfectly decorated and attended by the four constituent hosts of his military array, and by the great body of the priesthood . . . repaired to the great Bodhi-tree which was decorated with every variety of ornament, laden with flowers of every hue. A body of a thousand priests with the chief Thero (son of Moggali) at their head and a body of thousand monarchs with this emperor (Asoka) at their head having enclosed the sovereign himself as well as the great Bo-tree, with uplifted clasped hands gazed on the great Bo-tree," p. 112.

This extensive agreement in so many details, in these two accounts which are drawn from widely different sources, can scarcely be accidental. On the contrary, they seem to establish the identity of the two persons in question almost beyond doubt.

## APPENDIX IX.

# Dr. T. Bloch's Translation of the Inscription in Jain Temple at (Kamaldah) Pātaliputra.

*Text.*

संबत् १८४८ वर्षे मार्गशिर वदि ५ सोमवासरे श्रीपाडलीपुरवास्तव्य श्रीसकलसंघसमुदायेन श्रीस्थूलभद्रस्वामिजीप्रसादस्य[1] कारापितं कार्य्यस्यायं सूरौ[2] श्रीतपागच्छीय श्राद्धःलोढा श्रीगुलावचंदजी प्रतिष्ठितं सकलसूरिभिः ।

*Translation.*

In the year 1848, on the 5th day of the bright half of Mārgaśiras, a Monday,[3] the beginning of the building of the temple of the illustrious *Sthūlabhadra-svāmi-jī* was made by the whole congregation living at *Pāḍalipura;*[4] it was consecrated by the Sūri, the illustrious *Gulābcand-jī* of the *Tapāgaccha* (the son of) *Śrāiḥ Loḍhā* (?),[5] together with all the Sūris.

---

[1] Read प्रासादस्य

[3] Read सूरि

[3] The date is irregular. Assuming that *somavāsare* 'Monday' has been wrongly put for *saumya-vāsare* 'Wednesday,' the corresponding European date would be, Wednesday, 17th November, 1791 A.D. But the year may also be wrong, and intended either for 1849 or 1847, in which cases the European equivalents would be either Monday, 4th December 1792, or Monday, 8th December 1789.

[4] Professor Rhys Davids reads the third letter as ṭ making the word *Pāṭalipura.*

[5] I am very uncertain as to the meaning of these four syllables.—T. B.

B. S. Press—4917J—300—12 8.1908—W. M. D'C.

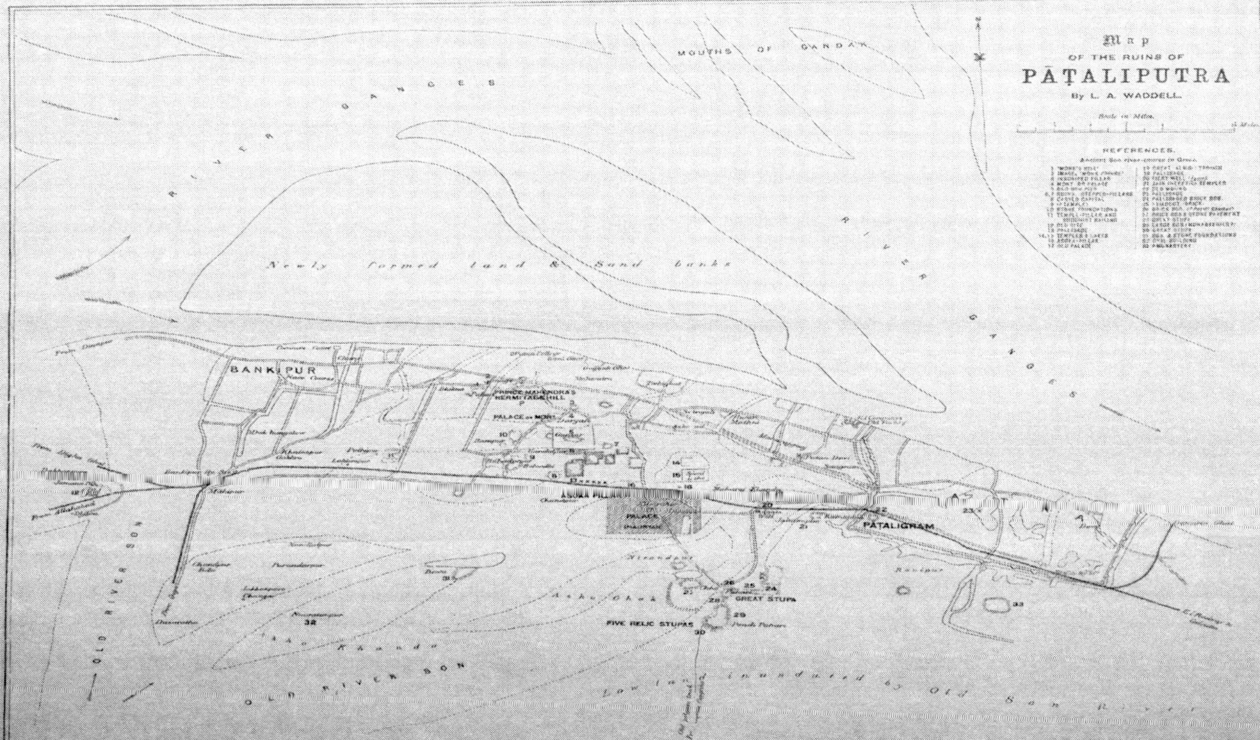
Map
OF THE RUINS OF
PĀṬALIPUTRA
By L. A. WADDELL.
Scale in Miles.
REFERENCES.
MOUTHS OF GANDAK
RIVER GANGES
Newly formed land & Sand banks
BANKIPUR
PRINCE MAHENDRA'S HERMITAGE HILL
PALACE of MORI
ASOKA PILLAR
PALACE
PĀTALIGRAM
GREAT STUPA
FIVE RELIC STUPAS
OLD RIVER SON
Low land inundated by Old Son River